CABINET OFFICE
OFFICE of the MINISTER
for the CIVIL SERVICE

Understanding Stress:

Part One

London: HMSO

ISBN 0 11 430019 4

ISBN 0 11 430019 4

Contents

Introduction

This book has been prepared for the Training Division of the Cabinet Office (OMCS) as part of the series *Understanding Stress.*

The series consists of four books:

- *Understanding Stress – Part One*
- *Understanding Stress – Part Two: Line Manager's Guide*
- *Understanding Stress – Part Three: Trainer's Guide*
- *Understanding Stress – Part Four: Welfare Officer's Guide*

The series has been produced as a resource and working tool to assist all those who have an interest in stress, either from their own point of view or from the point of view of someone who works with or manages other people.

Background

Stress as a likely cause of illness, problems and personal misery is giving rise to growing public as well as medical and scientific concern.

It is fair to say that at this point the complete scientific and clinical link between stress and illness has not been proved to the satisfaction of all parties. Despite this there is a growing realization that stress is an increasing problem.

The Economist noted that Britain is losing two per cent of its GNP per annum as a result of losses caused by stress-related diseases. This is a staggering figure which does not include less measurable costs such as human misery, lower efficiency and productivity.

In 1978 it was reported that Britain had one of the worst death rates from heart disease and strokes in the world – they account for 80,000 premature deaths per year.

Throughout this book and the others in the series the word 'stress' is used in the sense of the 'distress' which people experience from too many pressures and strains or too few challenges and stimuli. 'Distress' is something which occurs to all of us as does happiness. It is only where there is too much distress, physical or mental, that problems start.

Each individual responds differently to stress and each one of us has a different tolerance to it. In addition, the interplay between different causes of stress can be very different for different people.

All these books will be based on the relationships in the following model:

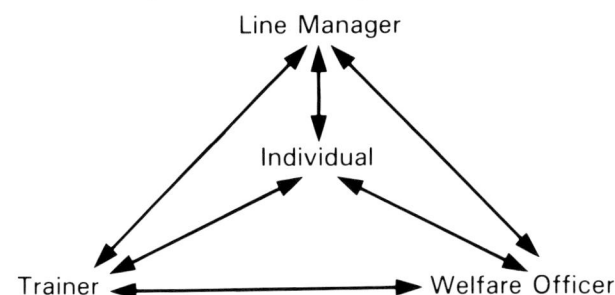

About this book

This book is divided into six discrete sections:

- Section 1. What is stress?
- Section 2. Symptoms of stress
- Section 3. Causes of stress
- Section 4. Managing stress
- Section 5. Further sources of help
- Section 6. Bibliography and details of stress studies

In Sections 1 to 4, text printed in black is designed to:

- synthesize existing material on the subject matter
- present this in non-technical and simple, accessible, language
- encapsulate key concepts
- provide a key information or teaching point

while text printed in blue is designed to:

- focus thought
- help people relate the basic information to their own circumstances
- supply leads to further information with selections from the main bibliography at the back of the book, and giving page/chapter references as appropriate
- provide space for the reader's notes

What's in it for you?

This book has been designed to be read and used from several different viewpoints:

- **the Individual** who wants to learn more about stress, its effects on them and to manage it
- **the Line Manager** interested in decreasing their own stress and that of their staff
- **the Trainer** interested in their own stress and that of their trainees
- **the Welfare Officer** interested in their own stress and that of their clients

The Individual

The information contained in the first four sections of the book will help you to:

- understand what stress is
- identify your personal stressors and stress levels
- identify coping mechanisms appropriate to you
- plan future methods of decreasing stress

The Line Manager

The Line Manager can use the information in the first four sections to:

- understand stress and how it affects people
- identify likely work-associated stressors
- plan strategies for decreasing work-related stress
- coach and counsel individuals who work for them
- take steps to manage personal stress

Further specific help and information is provided in *Understanding Stress – Part Two: Line Manager's Guide*

The Trainer

Using this book will help the Trainer to:

- understand stress and how it affects people
- identify likely work-associated stressors
- plan strategies for decreasing work-related stress
- coach and counsel individuals who work for them
- take steps to manage personal stress

The layout of the book provides further help for trainers in that the material:

- can be photocopied to be used as handouts or overhead projector slides
- used as discussion guides
- used as session notes

Further specific help, eg:

- useful organizations
- list of training materials
- sample programmes
- sample handouts etc

is provided in *Understanding Stress – Part Three: Trainer's Guide*

The Welfare Officer

The book will help the Welfare Officer to:

- identify likely causes of stress for themselves and their clients
- appreciate the role of the Line Manager and Trainer in dealing with stress
- plan to decrease work-associated stresses
- appreciate the proactive nature of their role in stress management and prevention
- prepare input sessions for courses
- run discussion sessions

Further specific advice and information is provided in *Understanding Stress – Part Four: Welfare Officer's Guide*

Acknowledgements

This and the other three books in the series *Understanding Stress* were developed for the Training Division of the Cabinet Office (OMCS) by Diane Bailey and Clare Sproston of Diane Bailey Associates, 4 Rochbury Close, Bamford, Rochdale OL11 5JF.

The authors would like to thank the following who helped them in preparing the series *Understanding Stress* by providing information and advice and giving permission to include material:

Trainers, Welfare Officers and others in Civil Service departments

Chief Superintendent Allison, New Scotland Yard
Angela Stern Associates
Meg Bond and James Kilty, University of Surrey
City Relaxation Counselling
Eleanor MacDonald Courses Ltd
Industrial Society (Pepperell Unit)
Jean Jackson
Murray Giles Associates
Dr Nimenko, Devonshire Clinic
Alistair Ostell, Occupational Psychology Management Centre, Bradford University
Rank-Xerox
Rochdale Health Authority
Dr Adrian Semmence, Civil Service Occupational Health Service
Stress Foundation

Special thanks to those departments who helped by sharing the development costs of the series:

Ministry of Agriculture, Fisheries and Food
Cabinet Office (OMCS) – Training Division and Personnel Management Division 2
Civil Service College
Department of Education and Science
Department of Employment
Department of Employment (Unemployment Benefit Service)
Office of Fair Trading
Foreign and Commonwealth Office
Department of Health and Social Security
Department of National Savings
HM Land Registry
Inland Revenue
Lord Chancellor's Department
National Environment Research Council
Office of Population Censuses and Surveys
Science and Engineering Research Council
Welsh Office

Section 1.
What is stress?

Contents

Using this section

This section can be used in two ways:

- If you are new to the subject of stress you will find it helpful to read through the whole section

- On the other hand you may find it useful to dip into this section as a reminder. For example, you may want to use one of the questionnaires for yourself or with colleagues

To help you dip into, or skim read, the material, each topic has a clear heading and the **Key point** is picked out in bold type.

By the time you have completed this section you will be able to:

- define what stress is

- understand why people react differently to the same stressors

- differentiate between healthy and unhealthy stress

- describe and recognize the three stages of the stress response

- understand the importance of getting the balance right between the individual and the environment

- recognize the extremes of types of behaviour responses to stressors

Where appropriate, reading relevant to the subject matter is listed for your information.

Defining stress

What is stress? Ten years ago we talked about the 'rat race'. Today we talk of the 'stress of modern living'. When we try to be specific it is often difficult for us to be precise about what we mean by stress. But it is important that we do reach a common understanding before we can begin to tackle the problem. Let's begin by examining what stress is – and what it is not.

Is stress distress?

Most of us tend to think that stress only occurs as a result of something unpleasant happening to us: we don't get an expected promotion; a long-standing relationship breaks up. Events like these are seen to be distressful. And, indeed they may be. The problem is that this is only one side of the coin. We may actually be relieved when we don't get a promotion because we are unsure of our ability to cope at a higher level. The breakup of our relationship may bring to an end a situation which was making us very unhappy. So, the result is not *distressful* – but it may still be *stressful.*

Action and reaction

Why is it that both happy and sad events have the same potential to cause stress? In physics, stress is defined as 'a force producing a change in the shape of a body'. A car for example may remain static until we apply a force by turning on the engine so that it can move. We can apply exactly the same principle to human stress. Something happens to us which causes our situation to change and demands us to readjust to a new situation. What causes the stress – the stressor – is immaterial. What does matter is the *degree* of readjustment which has to take place.

Definition

If we agree that:

● stress is a stimulus which causes a response

● that the stimulus can be perceived as both positive and negative

● it is the extent of the response which is important

then perhaps we can usefully define stress as 'a response made by people to demands made upon them'. Just what form that response can take will be examined in later pages.

Stress is a response made by people to demands made upon them

Ask yourself

Line Manager

● What have I asked my staff to do in the last week?

● Is anything I have asked them to do likely to cause a change in their working practices?

Trainer

● When I act as tutor, do I consider that for some people being on a course can be a very stressful situation?

Welfare Officer

● Do I ever give advice which asks people to change their life-style?

● Do I consider the effects this may have on them, other than a change in life-style?

For all of us

● What has happened to me recently – good or bad – which has meant a change in the way I go about my life?

● How do I feel about this?

Your notes/personal points

Selected reading

SELYE, H. *Stress without distress.* Chapter 1.
MADDERS, J. *Stress and relaxation.* Chapter 1.

Understanding the stress response

In the last section, we said that stress was a response made by people to demands made, either at work or in private life. All of us have different demands made upon us every day: to get to work on time; to meet a deadline; to prepare a meal for our children. We can't avoid these demands, which means that every day we are faced with a potentially stressful situation. So is stress necessarily a 'bad' thing? Of course it isn't – we all need to be able to respond to survive – indeed the body automatically provides a 'fight or flight' response to a perceived threat. (See page 9 for more information.)

Maintaining our equilibrium

If stress is a normal reaction to events, why do we think it is a problem? When we say that someone is suffering from stress what we mean is that they are under extra and excessive stress. Too many demands, or too few, are being made and they feel unable to cope.

It is rather like food – we all need to eat to stay alive, but too much or too little food both result in our becoming unwell. So it is with stress: too few demands may be as bad as too many. Someone who is doing an undemanding job – on a production line perhaps – may well find that this is as stressful for them as busy executives find their work. The result is the same in both cases, because the body's normal equilibrium is disturbed. We all need a certain amount of stress to survive, but when the balance is wrong we're in trouble.

Stress and the individual

If we all need a certain amount of stress to survive, does this mean that we all need the same amount or that we all respond to the same events in the same way? Of course it doesn't – everyone's response will be different because we are all unique. We are formed as a result of our genes, our experiences and our environment. A person who is brought up to be a high achiever may find it easier to cope with the pressures of an executive role than someone whose expectations were in another direction, and vice versa. That's why some of us thrive in situations which others find totally overwhelming. What is important is the degree of adaptation we have to make to a situation which determines whether we react positively or negatively – and find ourselves either going forward or failing to cope.

Each individual has a different response to stress

Ask yourself

Line Manager

- Am I asking too much/too little of my staff?
- Do I know how each individual is likely to react to an increase, or decrease, in workload/responsibility?

Trainer

- Do I ever ask Line Managers how they think an individual will respond to demands made on training courses?
- Have I considered changing the approach or methods I use when I know that a particular technique is likely to cause excessive stress?

Welfare Officer

- Do I spend enough time finding out about the person who is in difficulty?
- Do I ever assume that because I like/dislike a situation, then my clients will have the same response?

For all of us

- What sort of demands do I respond to positively at work?
- Do I work better under pressure?

___

Your notes/personal points

___

Selected reading

HARRIS, A. B. *Breakpoint: Stress and the crisis of modern living.* Chapter 4.

___

Fight or flight?

We said earlier that the body automatically produces a fight or flight response to threat. What actually happens to the body during this response? and why does it happen? We agreed that people have different perceptions of stressful events — what is stressful to you may not be so to your colleague. But whenever we do find a situation stressful, then we all respond in the same way. When we are faced with danger, the automatic primary stress response (fight or flight) is activated. This is a reflex bodily reaction designed to ensure that we can respond appropriately to danger – and, hopefully, survive.

The reaction

As soon as danger is recognized – a car crash, attack etc – the body is given an extra energy boost to get us out of danger, perhaps by fighting or by running away, depending on the circumstances. A message of red alert is sent to the brain which initiates dramatic changes in the hypothalamus. This is the control centre which integrates our reflex reactions and co-ordinates the different activities of our bodies. When the hypothalamus is activated, our muscles, brain, lungs and heart are given priority over any other bodily activity.

The sympathetic and parasympathetic nervous systems

The automatic primary stress response is a reflex action of the sympathetic nervous system. The message of danger is received and passed on to all parts of the body which prepares itself for vigorous physical action – fight or flight. Once the danger has passed, the parasympathetic nervous system takes over again and our bodies return to a state of equilibrium, usually called homeostasis, where all our functions are in balance.

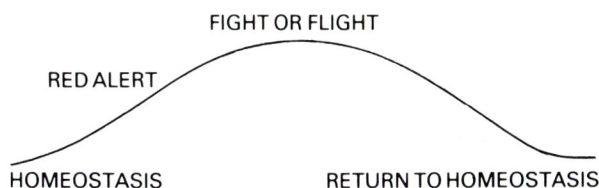

The diagram shows the stress response curve to danger. On page 11 we shall look at the actual changes that occur to our bodies to enable us to respond.

Fight or flight is the automatic reaction of the body to a perceived danger

Ask yourself

Line Manager

- Are there any potentially dangerous situations caused by the work that my staff do?
- Is the work done by my staff particularly hazardous or dangerous at any point?
- What circumstances in my own work could give rise to a fight or flight reaction?

Trainer

- In specific instances where people's work is potentially dangerous, how can I best prepare them?

Welfare Officer

- Are there certain groups of people in my department whose work is more likely to lead to danger than others?
- Do I know what other departments are doing in similar circumstances?

For all of us

- Are there any situations resulting from my work likely to lead to a fight or flight reaction, eg traffic accidents, physical attack?

Your notes/personal points

Selected reading

MADDERS, J. *Stress and relaxation.* p 17.

Stress and distress

Without some stress in our lives we could not survive. It is a natural part of life and is the way our bodies respond to demands. We all have an optimum level of stress where there is a healthy balance between ourselves and our environment. Selye identified four types of stress to show this balance:

- OVERSTRESS (too much stress)
- UNDERSTRESS (too little stress)
- EUSTRESS (good stress, balance right)
- DISTRESS (bad stress)

Selye suggests that we all need to find our own eustress without distress – that is to recognize within ourselves when we are in balance and when our bodies are telling us that 'enough is enough'.

Overstress and understress

Most of us dislike equally too much stress and too little stress. Both have an equal capacity to cause distress. It's just like making a curry; too much chilli powder and we won't be able to eat it, too little and it will be unpleasantly bland. But the optimum level of spicing depends upon our own individual tastes. In many ways stress is very similar – we could call it the 'spice of life'. Too much or too little both lead to distress.

Healthy and unhealthy stress

Nixon said that there were distinct signs of healthy and unhealthy stress.*

Healthy	Unhealthy
energetic	insomnia
adaptable	anxiety
approachable	aggressive
relaxed	defensive

Although this list is brief it does serve to give us some guidelines as to when our own personal stress levels are getting out of balance. You can read more about the signs of stress a little later under the heading, 'Symptoms of stress'.

Stress is the spice of life

*NIXON, P. G. F. 'Stress, lifestyle and cardio-vascular disease: A cardiological odyssey' in *British Journal of Holistic Medicine*. 1984, No. 1.

Ask yourself

Line Manager

- Do working conditions cause my staff too much or too little stress?
- What improvements can I make?

Trainer

- Can I design my training events to achieve positive use of stress?
- Am I aware of my own stress levels?

Welfare Officer

- Could any of the problems referred to me be caused by inappropriate levels of stress?
- Can I liaise with Line Managers or Trainers to improve inappropriate conditions?

For all of us

- Am I suffering too much, or too little, stress?
- Do I recognize my own eustress?

Your notes/personal points

Selected reading

NIXON, P. G. F. 'Stress, lifestyle and cardio-vascular disease' in *British Journal of Holistic Medicine*. pp 20–29.

Fight or flight: bodily changes

The purpose of the primary stress response is to prepare the body to respond to a perceived danger. It is unconscious and instantaneous. Without it we would be unable to survive. This is what happens:

- the brain goes on red alert and stimulates hormonal changes, including the production of the 'stress hormones' adrenalin and noradrenalin

- muscles tense ready for action

- the pupils of the eye dilate so we can see the danger more clearly

- the heart beats faster to get extra blood to our tense muscles and this raises blood pressure

- the extra blood for our muscles means that we need more oxygen and so we breathe more quickly

- the liver releases glucose to provide extra energy for our muscles

- our digestive systems shut down so our mouths go dry and our sphincters close

- we sweat in anticipation of expending extra energy

- our immune system slows

You can see from this list of reactions that the fight or flight response is highly complex but very necessary to give us extra energy to face danger. Once the danger has passed we will take some time to return to a state of homeostasis. We may pant and feel nauseous and will probably want to sit down and relax until we feel in balance again.

Complex bodily reactions occur in response to perceived danger

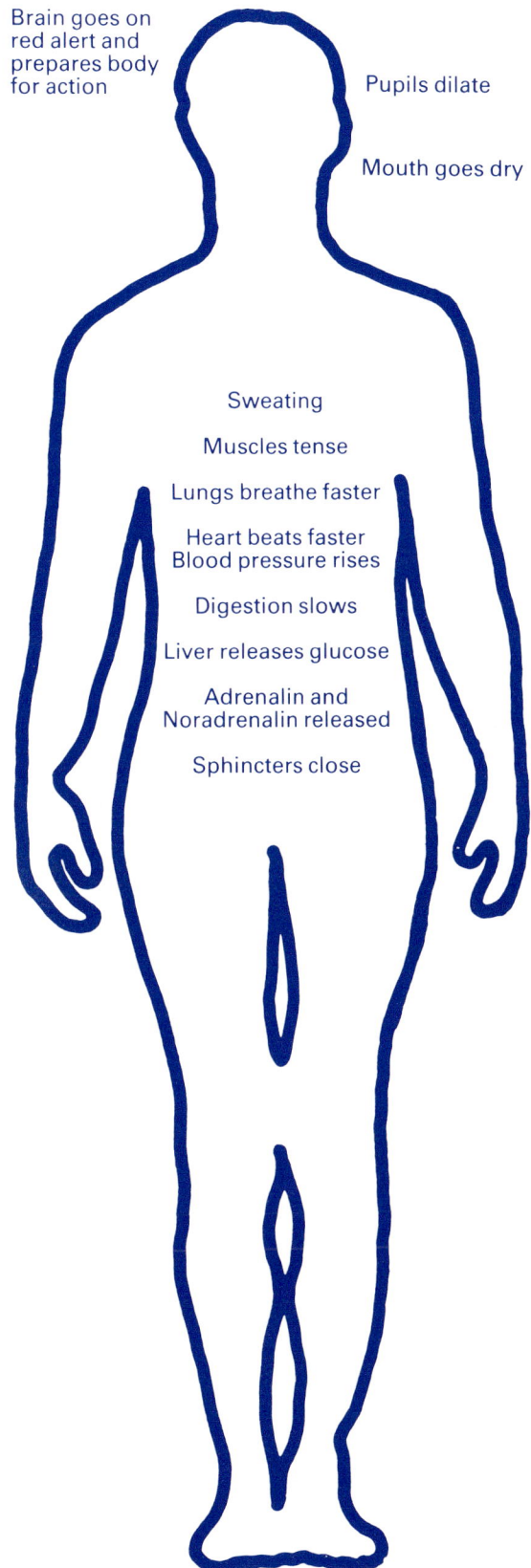

Brain goes on red alert and prepares body for action

Pupils dilate

Mouth goes dry

Sweating

Muscles tense

Lungs breathe faster

Heart beats faster
Blood pressure rises

Digestion slows

Liver releases glucose

Adrenalin and Noradrenalin released

Sphincters close

Selected reading

HARRIS, A. B. *Breakpoint: Stress and the crisis of modern living.* Appendix 1.

Secondary stress response

Some stress as part of everyday life is essential. It keeps us alert and ready to face the dangers of life. Without the fight or flight reaction we would not survive. It is a wholly good reaction – providing we are are allowed sufficient time to recover and regain our equilibrium. Unfortunately this does not always happen. And many of us find ourselves in situations where we cannot escape, so we experience a continual series of stress triggers. That's when the next stage, the secondary stress response begins, and we are heading for trouble, because frequent surges of stress hormones activate our bodies to run from things which we can't escape from.

Stress triggers

All sorts of things will cause us to have an inappropriate stress response. It may be travelling on a crowded and late train; being stuck in a traffic jam or even a constantly crying baby. We want to change the situation but we can't. Our bodies and brains still react to circumstances by activating the primary stress response, and then go on releasing *more* chemicals as it becomes evident that the initial reaction wasn't enough to get us out of danger. Stress triggers vary from person to person but perhaps the common denominator between them all is that we feel pressured and hemmed in.

What happens

When we feel that we have to do something and we can't escape, our body needs extra energy to cope. The energy provided by the primary stress response – the release of adrenalin and glucose – is not enough. So our body calls upon more powerful chemicals – cortico steroids – which like adrenalin, prepare us for action. At the same time the fats and sugars in our bodies are broken down and released into the bloodstream to give us more energy. As we become more and more unable to cope with the circumstances which have led to the reaction so more and more of our energy stores are depleted. Eventually our bodies are exhausted and we enter the third and most dangerous stage of stress – exhaustion.

The secondary stress response is activated as a result of demands from which we cannot escape.

General Adaptation Syndrome

As we have seen, stress falls into three separate stages:

- the fight or flight reaction
- the secondary stress reaction
- the third reaction – exhaustion

Selye described this as the General Adaptation Syndrome and related it to the three stages of life – childhood, adulthood and senility. He called the three stages:

- the alarm reaction
- the stage of resistance
- the stage of exhaustion

The diagrams on the following pages show why continual exposure to demands or stressors is harmful.

Effects of prolonged stress

The secondary stress response releases fats, sugars and steroids to give us extra energy – in situations where we cannot expend that energy. In addition the cortico steroids shut down those bodily activities which help us to develop and to resist disease, so that we have still more energy reserves to call on. As a result fats and sugars are concentrated in the blood, which can clog up and damage our arteries and so lead to heart disease. If you look back at the diagram on page 11 you can see why continual stress responses will also result in other illnesses, including stomach disorders and aching muscles. If we are able to exercise so that we can burn off the extra fats and sugars then we may be able to cope with this stage. It is only when we are continually exposed to demands and make no effort to discharge the effects that we fall into the third and most dangerous stage of stress response – and serious illness results. While we cannot say how long each stage takes, because this will vary from person to person, we do know that all of us will all move through the stages unless we cope with or remove the stressor.

Prolonged exposure to stressors is harmful to the body

Your notes/personal points

Selected reading

BOOTH, A. L. *Stressmanship.* pp 34–41.

The three stages of the stress response

The response	What happens	The effect
FIGHT OR FLIGHT	Red alert. Body and brain prepare for action, extra energy released.	Response to danger, meet it and return to equilibrium.
SECONDARY	Fats, sugars and cortico steroids released for more energy.	Unless extra fats etc used up then third stage moved into.
EXHAUSTION	Energy stores used up.	Serious illness leading to death.

The three phases of the General Adaptation Syndrome

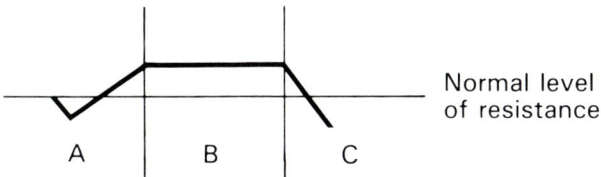

Normal level of resistance

A   B   C

A. **Alarm reaction** The body shows the changes characteristic of the first exposure to the stressor. At the same time, its resistance is diminished and, if the stressor is sufficiently strong (severe burns, extremes of temperature), death may result.

B. **Stage of resistance** Resistance ensues if continued exposure to the stressor is compatible with adaptation. The bodily signs characteristic of the alarm reaction have virtually disappeared, and resistance ensues.

C. **Stage of exhaustion** Following long-continued exposure to the same stressor, to which the body has become adjusted, eventually adaptation energy is exhausted. The signs of alarm reaction reappear, but now they are irreversible, and the individual can suffer permanent damage (even die).

Your notes/personal points

Selected reading

SELYE, H. *Stress without distress.* pp 35–44.

The individual and the environment

When we talk about the 'environment' we mean the particular circumstances in which we live. Everyone's environment will be different. It will include such things as:

- where we work
- where we live
- our family
- our friends
- our life-style
- our beliefs
- our education
- our attitudes

All these things, and others, form our total environment. Stress becomes distress when there is a misfit between

- what we want and are capable of doing
- what our environment offers and demands of us

This is called the Person: Environment fit. It emphasises that it is the importance of achieving the *right balance* between the person (P) and the environment (E) which will decide whether we are healthily or unhealthily stressed.

Moving forward

So far we have said that the body responds healthily to stress when it meets a challenge and then returns to the state of equilibrium called homeostasis. It is important to realise though that the right balance may be one where we have learnt to cope with a situation and have adapted to it in such a way that our personal 'steady state' has moved up a notch. So stress can also be seen as a stimulus to personal growth. Most of us at one time or another have started a new job and, at first, felt unable to cope with the new demands and pressures of the work. After a time we learnt what the job entailed and how to do it, and it was no longer distressful. We probably began to enjoy it and maybe to look for more stimulus, eg promotion. What has happened is that we have changed our homeostasis level, but, because there is still a fit between ourselves and our environment and we have adapted to the uncertainty, we do not become distressed.

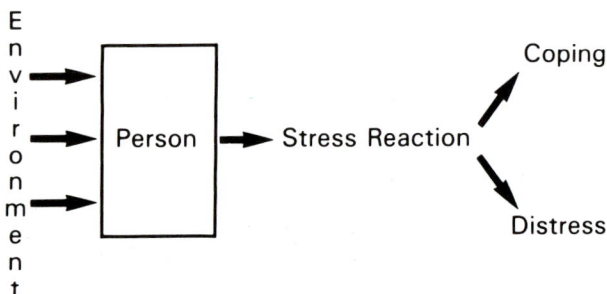

Ask yourself

Line Manager

- Do I consider the people who work for me against their total environment?
- Do I know of any forthcoming work events or changes which may prove stressful until we can all cope with them?

Trainer

- Do I make my training environment as free from inappropriate stress as possible?
- What changes, if any, should I make?
- Do I accept that stress can aid the learning process?

Welfare Officer

- What can I do to minimize stressors in the work environment?
- Do I keep up to date with changes in work patterns and job demands?

For all of us

- Am I aware how the factors of my environment fit together?
- Are there any particular factors which are causing problems?

Your notes/personal points

Selected reading

BEEHR, T. A. and BHAGAT, R. S. (ed.) *Human stress and cognition in organisations:* An integrated perspective. pp 6–13.

Type 'A' behaviour

We have seen that stress is acceptable when there is a balance between who we are and the pressures of our environment. Stress is necessary so that we can move forward to meet and overcome the challenges in our lives. Stress only becomes unacceptable when we fail to meet those challenges. However, it appears from recent research, that some people push themselves into a state of distress by their behaviour and life-style. It is almost as if they are unwilling to accept that they have a personal limit beyond which they should not go.

In 1974, Dr Meyer Friedman published the results of ten years research into heart disease. He concluded that it was *behaviour* which was the single most important factor as to whether an individual would suffer from coronary heart disease (CHD). Those he termed Type 'A' people were almost three times more likely to get CHD than the Type 'B' people. What are the characteristics of Type 'A' behaviour?

Characteristics of Type 'A' behaviour

Insecurity of status
Regardless of how other people perceive them, Type 'A' people never quite feel that they have achieved enough, so they are always struggling to get that little bit further.

Hyperaggressiveness
Type 'A's exhibit more than ambition – they have a ruthless streak to achieve and dominate.

Permanent hostility
Always present in Type 'A's – it is the sort of anger that manifests itself as the result of (mostly) trivial events.

Hurry sickness
Trying to fit in more than time allows, perhaps by doing two things at once.

Drive to self-destruction
Shown by very severe Type 'A's – a feeling that if they continue to push themselves then eventually their own bodies will relieve the pressure by succumbing to serious illness.

In addition to these five common characteristics, Dr Friedman also identified three secondary characteristics:

- a precise and quantified way of thinking and speaking

- difficulty in using similes and metaphors

- difficulty in developing imagery in thought and speech

A continual struggle

Overall we can best describe Type 'A' people as those who are in a continual state of struggle and never learn to balance the P:E fit. Consequently they are prone to stress-related disease and, ultimately, to CHD.

Type 'A' people are likely to show signs of distress

Ask yourself

Line Manager

- Do I recognize any of these characteristics
    - in me?
    - in my staff?

Trainer

- Do I run any courses where it might be useful to build in a discussion on stress-prone behaviour?

- Would it be useful to 'build in' stressors to some courses to produce a desired result?

Welfare Officer

- Do any of my current clients exhibit signs of Type 'A' behaviour?

- Does anyone in the section (including myself) show signs of Type 'A' behaviour?

For all of us

- Can I recognise in myself what is
    - acceptable stress?
    - unacceptable stress?

___

Your notes/personal points

___

Selected reading

FRIEDMAN, M. and ULMER, D. *Treating Type 'A' behaviour: You and your heart.* Chapter 3.

Type 'B' behaviour

When we look at the characteristics of Type 'A' people it might seem that they lead the sort of lives which would make them interesting and likely to succeed. By contrast, perhaps we secretly think that to be a Type 'B' person would be to be dull and mundane. Perhaps it's a symptom of 20th century life that makes us feel that we have to appear competitive and striving – not to do so might seem 'wimpish'. But are Type 'B's like this, or is there more to them?

Characteristics of Type 'B' behaviour

Ability to take a long view
Unlike 'A's, Type 'B' people don't try to 'over-egg the pudding'. They don't try to meet unrealistic targets or to take on more than they can cope with. Often they are better at delegating. They don't expect a task to be done *exactly* as they would do it – but they do trust their subordinates to accomplish it.

Speed is not the issue
Type 'B's are not clock-watchers, and are secure enough within themselves not to complete every task to deadline. Whatever they do they give their full attention to it.

Sense of personal identity
They don't feel that they have to earn respect and love, but are secure in who they are and what they do. They take into account not what may be, but what was and what is.

Sense of proportion
The constant struggle and anger of the Type 'A' is wholly foreign to Type 'B's. They always maintain a sense of balance at events in their lives.

Somewhere in between
Most people will fall somewhere between the two extreme types described.

The two extremes

Friedman's work gives us some insight into why some people are more prone to stress-related disease. It needs to be emphasised that Type 'A' and Type 'B' behaviour can only be seen as a yardstick – there are no absolutes. However, if you recognize that you are prone to 'A' personality factors then it may be worthwhile looking for ways to modify your behaviour. Have a go at the questionnaires on the next pages to help you assess which type of behaviour is dominant in you.

Type 'B' people are less likely to show signs of distress

Ask yourself

Line Manager

- Do I believe that more is better?
- Am I really concerned with deadlines?

Trainer

- How can I persuade trainees that Type 'B' behaviour is less damaging?

Welfare Officer

- Can I recognize the square peg in the round hole?
- Will I, if necessary, recommend a transfer or a posting?

For all of us

- Do I respond to pressure by behaving uncharacteristically?

Your notes/personal points

Selected reading

FRIEDMAN, M. and ULMER, D. *Treating Type 'A' behaviour: You and your heart.* Chapter 5.

Who are you?

Circle the number which you feel most closely represents your own behaviour.

Never late	5	4	3	2	1	0	1	2	3	4	5	Casual about appointments
Anticipates what others are going to say (nods, interrupts, finishes for them)	5	4	3	2	1	0	1	2	3	4	5	Good listener
Always rushed	5	4	3	2	1	0	1	2	3	4	5	Never feels rushed (even under pressure)
Impatient while waiting	5	4	3	2	1	0	1	2	3	4	5	Can wait patiently
Goes all out	5	4	3	2	1	0	1	2	3	4	5	Casual
Tries to do many things at once, thinks what they are about to do next	5	4	3	2	1	0	1	2	3	4	5	Takes one thing at a time
Emphatic in speech (may pound desk)	5	4	3	2	1	0	1	2	3	4	5	Slow, deliberate talker
Wants good job recognized by others	5	4	3	2	1	0	1	2	3	4	5	Cares about satisfying themselves no matter what others may think
Fast (walking, eating etc)	5	4	3	2	1	0	1	2	3	4	5	Slow in doing things
Hard-driving	5	4	3	2	1	0	1	2	3	4	5	Easy-going
Hides feelings	5	4	3	2	1	0	1	2	3	4	5	Expresses feelings
Few interests outside work	5	4	3	2	1	0	1	2	3	4	5	Many outside interests

Source: COOPER, C. L. and DAVIDSON, M. J. *Stress and the woman manager.* Martin Robertson. 1983

Selected reading

GILES, E. *Stress and the personnel director: A preliminary investigation.* pp 48–51.

Scoring the 'Who are you?' questionnaire

Each line can score a maximum of 11 points. The points being allocated as shown below. You score the points listed against the number you circled on the questionnaire. There are 12 lines, so the maximum score is 132 points and the minimum 12 points.

Number circled	5	4	3	2	1	0	1	2	3	4	5
	↓	↓	↓	↓	↓	↓	↓	↓	↓	↓	↓
Points	11	10	9	8	7	6	5	4	3	2	1

Who are you?

Once you have added up your total score you can find your behaviour tendency by comparing it with the table below.

Points		
	104 – 143	Extreme Type 'A'
	91 – 103	Type 'A'
	65 – 90	Type 'B'
	13 – 64	Extreme Type 'B'

A word of warning

As with all self-assessment questionnaires it is as well to take the results with a small pinch of salt – that is to see them as useful in indicating a tendency in your behaviour rather than an immutable fact. This point is highlighted by a study undertaken by Eileen Giles on personnel directors. She asked the respondents in her survey to answer the questionnaire and then asked an 'observer' – a person who was a close work colleague – to answer it on behalf of the respondent. When the results were compared she found that there were significant discrepancies between the individual answers, although it was still possible for the personnel directors and their observers to end up with the same score. She concluded that there were serious doubts about the validity of using this questionnaire as the sole basis for determining personality type.

Suggestion

Bearing the above in mind, you may find it helpful to ask someone who knows you well at work to complete the questionnaire on your behalf. Compare not only the total result but also the individual answers. You may find it very revealing.

Conclusion

Some stress is necessary for all of us to function effectively. It is only when too much or too little stress occurs that performance deteriorates.

Everyone has a different level of acceptable stress and finds different demands stressful. Overstress to one person is understress to someone else.

Stress results not only from major demands but also from an accumulation of minor demands. What is necessary is that we recognize that too much stress brings an inescapable result. In order to minimize the harmful effects of this result positive action is needed. Section 4 of this book deals with how to cope with stress.

Section 2.
Symptoms of stress

Contents

Using this section

This section can be used in two ways:

- If you are new to the subject of stress you will find it helpful to read through the whole section.

- On the other hand you will find it useful to dip into this section as a reminder. For example, you may want to use one of the questionnaires for yourself or with colleagues.

To help you dip into, or skim read, the material, each topic has a clear heading and the **Key point** is picked out in bold type.

By the time you have completed this section you will be able to:

- understand when stress can become dangerous to health

- recognize that everyone has a different tolerance level to stress

- recognize why our bodies react to stress

- identify the psychological, emotional and behavioural symptoms of stress

- identify the major and minor results on health of exposure to stress

- recognize when we and others are suffering from the effects of stress

- recognize when we and others are showing signs of stress at work

Where appropriate, reading relevant to the subject matter is listed for your information.

Is stress dangerous?

We have defined stress as a response made by people to demands made upon them. Obviously we all need a certain amount of stress in order to survive. If we were unable to respond to things which happen in our lives – good or bad – then we would lose our capacity to make decisions about the things which affect our lives. So some stress is essential.

But stress can become a dangerous response when there is either too little or too much, because our bodies are unable to adapt. Selye simply defined stress as 'the rate of wear and tear on the body'. Every time we are faced with a demand which requires a change in the pattern of our lives our minds and bodies have to respond to it and adapt to cope with it. Too many demands can lead to a breakdown although individual reactions vary.

Adaptive processes

To understand the way we constantly have to adapt, and why eventually it can become dangerous, it is useful to take the example of a car windscreen. If that windscreen is constantly exposed to the weather – hot in summer and freezing in winter – it eventually becomes weakened by that exposure. Eventually a minor incident, such as a pebble hitting the glass, can be enough to crack it into a thousand pieces. The same process happens to all glass, although the time-scale varies according to the strength of the glass.

Adaptation

Adaptive processes take place in people in the same way. Whatever the change – or stressor – the body responds instantly. The stressor can be physical (a change in the work environment) or emotional, (anger) but the body still attempts to maintain its equilibrium by responding. Sometimes that response will be all that is needed, we adjust very quickly and no damage is done. Sometimes our response is inadequate, or we have so many demands on us that our body is overwhelmed with the number of changes it is having to make. When that happens we are heading for danger and it may only take a minor incident to push us 'over the limit'.

Stress can be dangerous when we are asked to adapt to too many demands

Ask yourself

Line Manager

- Do any members of my staff seem to be having trouble coping with their work load?
- Can I do anything about this?

Trainer

- Am I up to date with the work demands made on the people I meet as trainees?
- How can I remain up to date?

Welfare Officer

- Am I aware of any change in the pattern of people coming to me for help?
- Are there any recent or expected changes in work patterns which may explain this situation?

For all of us

- Am I aware of too many demands being made on me?
- Am I finding it more difficult to adapt/respond to everyday demands.

Your notes/personal points

Selected reading

LEVI, L. *Stress in industry: Causes, effects and prevention.* pp 6–7.

Does stress result in change?

All of us are faced every day with situations which ask something of us. Often these demands are quite minor, but they still demand adaptation. Does that mean that it is inevitable that we will all, sooner or later, face a danger point and become ill? Luckily, most of us have learned coping skills which can help us to recognise and diminish the effects of stress. But we need to understand what happens physically and psychologically when we are faced with demands. In addition we need to understand why people we know very well may sometimes behave in a way which is out of character.

What happens

When a demand is made (the stressor) our bodies undergo a series of complex changes. Muscles tense, our brains instruct the adrenal glands to release the hormones adrenalin and noradrenalin, our pupils dilate and hearts pump more quickly. Other changes happen as well and you can find out more about these in the first section – 'What is stress'. But you can see that the response to a stressor is immediate and complex. Mostly we aren't even aware that all these things are happening to our bodies because the response is automatic rather than consciously willed.

Cause and effect

If the reactions by our bodies to stressors are a natural reflex, why do they matter? Perhaps the best way to answer this is to carry out a short experiment.
   Clench your right hand into a fist and hold your arm in the air for several minutes.
   How did you get on? Probably your arm started to ache and you may have had some difficulty unclenching your fist.
   If you imagine that happening to your muscles when they respond to stress you can quickly see that, if the stress is prolonged, permanent damage is likely to occur – and it's not just our muscles which react to stressors!

Every action has a reaction, many demands made on us can result in stress

Ask yourself

Line Manager

- Has anyone who works for me begun to behave in an unusual or out-of-character way?
- What can I do about this?

Trainer

- Do I really understand this subject?
- What exercises or other training material do I need to get the points across?

Welfare Officer

- Am I too concerned with the mechanics of the problem rather than their effects on the client?
- Should I liaise more closely with the client's line manager?

For all of us

- Am I aware of behaving differently?
- Am I more tense than normal?

Your notes/personal points

Selected reading

CHAITOW, L. *Your complete stress-proofing programme.* Chapter 2.

Degrees of stress

Some people react better to a stressor than others. That's because we all have different understandings of what constitutes a threat. For example, some of us would find it very stressful to be placed in a narrow, dark, confined space. Others of us positively enjoy potholing! Again, some people would go to pieces at the thought of speaking in public, while others make their living from it. So it is largely to do with ourselves and our make-up as to whether a situation will be stressful or not. Whatever that stressful situation is though, if we are constantly exposed to it then we are likely to do ourselves some permanent damage.

It's important that we recognise that not all demands will be stressful in the same way to everybody.

Stress is individual

Because we all have different perceptions of threat we can see that stress is not quite as simple as cause and effect. A china cup falling onto a concrete floor will always break. But we can't say that of people. A death in the family may affect different members of the family in a variety of ways. Some may be pleased or relieved – perhaps they disliked the person – while others will be plunged into despair. We should never fall into the trap of assuming that because we find a situation stressful everyone around us will have the same response. Nor should we believe that because we do not find something stressful that neither will other people.

Everyone has a different tolerance to demands – what is stressful to one may not be to another

Ask yourself

Line Manager

- How often do I put myself in the other person's shoes?
- Am I too task-orientated?

Trainer

- How often do I remember to see things from the trainee's point of view?
- Should I 'de-stress' my training sessions?

Welfare Officer

- How stressed do I get by the clients' problems?
- Which problems do I find most difficult to cope with?

For all of us

- What situations do I find worrying?
- What do I enjoy which people I know find worrying?

Your notes/personal points

Recognising stress responses

By being constantly exposed to demands our bodies are repeatedly attempting to adapt. Selye coined the term 'General Adaptation Syndrome' (GAS) to describe this process. Most of us can cope very well if we are not asked to take on too much. For example we deal with the unexpected death of a loved one by allowing ourselves to grieve – the natural response to this stressor. But if death is followed by our being made redundant and then getting divorced, we are likely to find ourselves facing a stress overload – and that can cause us serious damage. (See page 49 for the stress effect of various events.)

Symptoms as messages

When we ask our bodies to adapt to repeated stressors our general physical and emotional health declines. Our bodies are simply not able to cope with all we are asking, and disease occurs. The problem is that many of us are simply unaware that we are asking too much of ourselves – perhaps we are afraid to be seen as 'weak' and feel that we must 'keep going'. So we ignore the physical signs and hope that they will go away. Sometimes they will, particularly if we are able to alter the situation or remove ourselves from the stressor, perhaps by having a holiday. If such a major change is neither appropriate or possible you may find that to take a short walk, do a lot of gardening, etc will help. But if we continue to ignore the warning signs – the symptoms – then eventually we are heading for problems.

The adaptation stage

While most symptoms that appear during adaptation can be debilitating to some degree, they can be dealt with before they lead to real danger. How long the adaptation stage takes before we pass the point of no return will vary with each individual. Factors such as general health, support mechanisms (such as friends), and diet all play their part in determining when we will become exhausted and finally unable to cope. When we are no longer able to adapt then that is the point at which we can become ill – and perhaps seriously so.

Stress symptoms provide a message telling us to do something before it is too late

Ask yourself

Line Manager

- What would be my reaction to a member of my staff who said that they were under stress?
- Do I take stress seriously – both for myself and for my staff?
- Do I keep my eyes open for the physical indications and signs of stress?

Trainer

- How can I work towards getting people to recognise their responses to stress?
- Do I need resources other than those I have?

Welfare Officer

- Am I too concerned to find immediate solutions without helping the client adapt and cope?
- Do I recognise stress as a discrete problem?

For all of us

- Do I think it would be weak to admit to feeling stressed?
- Why is this?

_____

Your notes/personal points

_____

Physical stress symptoms

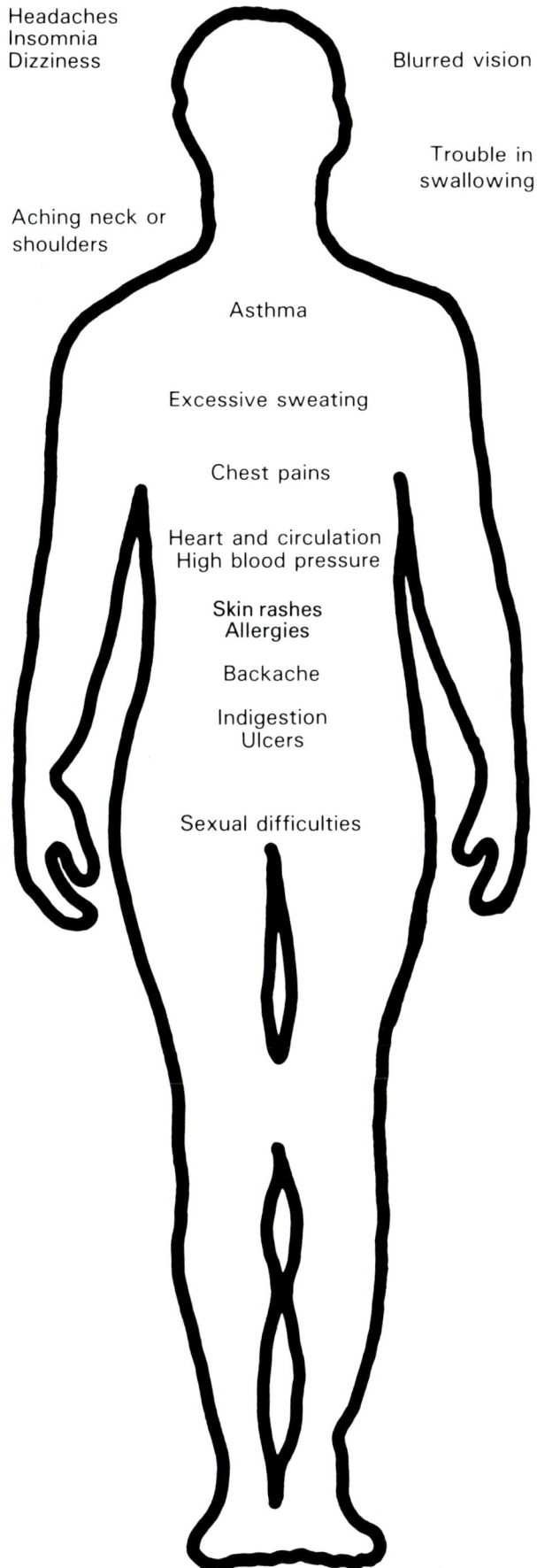

Headaches
Insomnia
Dizziness

Blurred vision

Trouble in
swallowing

Aching neck or
shoulders

Asthma

Excessive sweating

Chest pains

Heart and circulation
High blood pressure

Skin rashes
Allergies

Backache

Indigestion
Ulcers

Sexual difficulties

What are the symptoms of stress?

Virtually anything we do will produce a change in our bodies. If we go for a twenty-mile run the change will include such things as an accelerated heart beat, tired muscles and sweating. If we were fit to begin with, and rested properly after the run, then we would probably be alright. But if we weren't fit to begin with or refused to rest then it is possible that we could cause ourselves harm. So it is with stress symptoms. If you are asked to talk to a difficult client or meet a deadline then your heart will beat faster, your muscles tense and your breathing accelerate. It's easy to see from this example that if the stressor is prolonged you are probably going to end up with aching muscles and other symptoms of stress.

Physical symptoms

In the next few pages we'll be looking in detail at the physical, behavioural and psychological disorders associated with repeated exposure to stressors. For the moment though we can list some of the physical symptoms which you should be looking for when trying to assess if you are heading for permanent stress damage. They include: insomnia; high blood pressure; indigestion; heart problems.

Ask yourself

For all of us

- What physical symptoms of which I am currently aware are truly physical and which might be caused by stress?

Your notes/personal points

Selected reading

NORFOLK, D. *Executive stress.* p 16.

25

Major physical responses

When we look at the symptoms of stress and the illnesses that can result from repeated exposure to stressors it is tempting to put all disease and ill-health down to the effects of stress. And of course it is true that constant exposure to stressors will result in illness, either mental, physical or both. We do however need to remember that a great deal depends on the make-up of the individual. Our characters, genes, background and lifestyle will all have their effect on our susceptibility to disease. Nevertheless there is a link between constant stress and major illness, because the body's response to stress is to produce hormones which in turn activate the release of other changes in body chemistry and lessen the ability of our immune system to cope with disease.

Coronary heart disease

Coronorary heart disease (CHD) is the biggest killer in the western world. It is still more prevalent among men than women, but it is interesting that a study in 1980 by Haynes and Feinleib* revealed that working women with children were more likely to have CHD than those without children. Other studies have found a positive link between competitive, aggressive behaviour and CHD.

It is thought that because reaction to stressors increases the fat content in the blood that persistent stress gradually leads to these excess fats being deposited on the artery walls – eventually resulting in hardening of the arteries and the onset of CHD.

Cancer

There has been a good deal of research into the relationship between stress and cancer, and while, as yet, no firm conclusions can be drawn it does appear to be true that people who are prone to symptoms of stress, such as anger, fear and a feeling of helplessness are more susceptible to cancer. It therefore follows that it makes sense to fight cancer not only with recognized treatment – chemotherapy for example – but also to encourage sufferers to adopt a positive approach to tackling the disease rather than become overwhelmed by it.

Digestive disorders

The digestive system seems particularly prone to stressors. Some people often experience difficulty in swallowing when they are in a high tension situation – having lunch with a

prospective employer for example. Persistent indigestion is also indicative that we are stressed. More seriously, ulcers seem to have a direct relationship with stress.

Ulcers

One person in ten will get an ulcer at some time during their life, and every year millions of working days are lost because of them. A steroid called hydrocortisone is over-produced when we are emotionally disturbed, angry or upset. This has two effects: increased acids are produced in the stomach; and the mucosa which protect the stomach lining are reduced. This lack of protection combined with the extra acidity causes a breach in the wall – an ulcer. Ulcers can be treated by changing diets and by drugs but they are likely to recur if we continue to expose ourselves to the same stressors which led to them in the first place.

Diabetes

Adult onset diabetes is very common – and becoming more so in this country. It often follows an upset to the system – physical or emotional. It appears that when the adrenal system is activated by stressful circumstances this causes a reduction of insulin production so that the body is no longer able to convert sugar into glucose – and diabetes ensues.

Summary

It does appear that stress is implicated in a number of serious illnesses. While it would be foolish to say that removing stress will automatically enable us to live longer and more fulfilling lives, there is certainly enough evidence to suggest that if we ignore the relationship between the sort of lives we lead and disease then we do so at our peril.

Constant exposure to stressors can result in serious illness

Your notes/personal points

Selected reading

LEVI, L. *Stress in industry: Causes, effects and prevention.* pp 10–14.

---

*HAYNES, S. G. and FEINLEIB, M., 'Women, work and coronary heart disease' in *American Journal of Public Health.* Vol 70, 1980. pp 133–141.

Minor physical responses

Stressful situations give rise to a whole host of minor disorders which at best cause discomfort and at worst can lead to serious ill-health. Don't be tempted to think that just because these are not as obviously serious as coronary heart disease that they are not worth worrying about – they are! In this category we can include allergies, migraine, asthma, eczema, psoriasis and arthritis.

Headaches

Most of us at one time or another have suffered from a headache. Think back to a time when you had to maintain an alertness without being able to change your surroundings or position – driving a long distance or revising for an exam. That sort of experience causes muscle contraction in the scalp, forehead and neck – and so leads to a tension headache. It is relatively easy with simple massage to relax the muscles and remove the pain – and better for us than constantly resorting to aspirin.

Migraine

Migraine is different. Its cause is not so readily apparent, nor is it so readily cured. Migraine is often accompanied by nausea, and can affect the vision. Often it is so severe that the person is totally debilitated. People who suffer from migraine usually have an inborn tendency to migraine, but an attack is triggered by specific factors which can include stressors such as change or work overload. The stress hormones, adrenalin and noradrenalin, affect the blood vessels in the head. It is the constriction or dilation of these vessels that cause migraine. Avoidance and relaxation can reduce the likelihood of attacks.

Allergies

Allergies are extremely uncomfortable. They can result in breathing difficulties, rashes, itching and pain. Common allergies relate to foodstuffs – chocolate, milk, strawberries. Others relate to airborne substances – dust and pollen. It seems that every new discovery – inks, paper, cleaning fluid for example – increases the likelihood of someone somewhere developing an allergy. In one or two extreme cases it seems that just living in the twentieth century is a cause of allergy!

Is there a relationship between stressors and allergy? The answer seems to be a cautious 'yes'. When we respond to stressors the pituitary gland stimulates the production of mineral corticoids, and these have been directly related to allergy.

If you suffer from allergic responses, or you know someone who does, it may be a good idea to try and trace the onset of an allergic reaction beyond the immediate cause. You may find that you are more liable to succumb to an allergy when you have been through a particularly stressful time.

Skin disorders

Uncomfortable conditions such as eczema and psoriasis can also be exacerbated by stress, in the same way as allergies. Because the appearance of these disorders can be unpleasant they in turn become a source of stress – and the sufferer can become locked into a vicious circle. So it will be helpful if you suffer from these conditions not only to treat them medically but to look at the way you respond to them mentally, by tackling any stressors which are present in your life.

Arthritis

Often thought of as affecting only the elderly, in fact arthritis makes no age distinction. While the actual cause of arthritis is still not clear there is evidence to suggest that it can be triggered by stressful situations, so it is as important to treat the stress as it is to treat the disease.

Summary

All these illnesses, both major and minor are not solely the result of excessive and long-term stress in our environments. There is a relationship between them and the demands that are made on us. Dismissing stress as a cause of disease is just as absurd as correlating all illness with stress. We need to be aware that stress can act as a trigger – and that it is within all of us to take steps to ensure that the trigger is not pulled. In addition, stress can exacerbate existing problems.

Stress acts as a trigger for both major and minor illnesses

Ask yourself

- Am I suffering from any physical symptoms which may be stress-related?

Your notes/personal points

Selected reading

BOOTH, A. L. *Stressmanship.* Chapter 17.

Physical stress symptoms

Ask yourself

Line Manager

- Do I know how my staff will react to my demands?
- Do I temper my behaviour to the individual to reduce possible aggression and distress?
- Do I take serously that stressors can contribute to ill-health for both me and my staff?
- Do any members of my staff suffer regularly from any major or minor physical disorders?

Trainer

- Can I liaise more effectively with the occupational health service for professional input on courses?
- Do I understand the relationship between disease and stress?
- What techniques could I use on stress management courses to elicit symptoms from trainees in a safe and caring environment?

Welfare Officer

- Am I aware of national and local trends for coronary heart disease and other serious illness?
- How does my caseload compare with these norms?
- Do I liaise with the occupational health service for information on patterns of illness?
- Do I try to relate patterns of illness to demands made in the workplace?

_____

Your notes/personal points

_____

Selected reading

LEVI, L. *Stress in industry: Causes, effects and prevention.* pp 10–14.
MADDERS, J. *Stress and relaxation.* pp 115–116.

Other symptoms of stress

So far the symptoms identified as being precursors of stress-related disease have been very specific. We can all recognise when our backs are aching or when we've got indigestion. But these are not the only symptoms. There are others which are perhaps not so easy for us to recognise, although they may be indicative that we are asking too much of ourselves. Sometimes with these sorts of symptoms we need other people who know us well to act as a warning and let us know when we are heading for trouble.

These signs fall into two types:

- psychological and behavioural
- social

We'll be looking in detail at both of these later so for the moment it's only necessary to give a brief explanation.

Psychological/emotional and behavioural symptoms

When we no longer 'feel ourselves', are less energetic and more irritable.

Social symptoms

When we look for extra stimulus – such as through food, alcohol or in our sex lives.

This list is not intended to be comprehensive and you should not assume that having a symptom necessarily means that the cause is stress. However it may be, particularly if no other reason presents itself. Remember that if the cause *is* stress, then treating the symptom – like taking aspirin for a headache – may relieve it but won't remove it. Only changing the situation to a more acceptable one can do that.

The symptoms of stress are varied and include physical, mental and other changes

Ask yourself

Line Manager

- Have I noticed any increase in minor illnesses among my staff?
- Has the rate of absenteeism among my staff changed recently?

Trainer

- Do I do all I can to ensure a stress-free training environment?
- Do I give people enough time to get used to the new environment?

Welfare Officer

- Are there any discernible patterns in staff illness/absenteeism/resignation?
- Do I look for trends rather than just dealing with individual problems?

For all of us

- Am I drinking/smoking/eating more than normal?
- Can I change the situation which is causing me problems?

Your notes/personal points

Selected reading

NORFOLK, D. *Executive stress.* p 16.

Psychological, emotional and behavioural responses

At the psychological level our response to stress involves the arousal of various emotions and actions. These emotions include anxiety, guilt, depression and pessimism. The physical responses include those things which we may want to do rather than things that we are able to do – including running away or 'freezing'.

These sorts of reactions are initial attempts at coping with the stressor with which we are faced. Sometimes they can be the appropriate reaction and bring us safely through a difficult situation. Where they are unhealthy, though, is when we either become immersed in the feelings or when we try to suppress them. If we are angry because we didn't get the promotion we wanted, it is better to express anger rather than to allow a sense of injustice to fester inside our heads.

Depression

All of us at some time or other have felt depressed. In Britain 50 per cent of all people who are seen by a GP are treated for depressive illness. Perhaps it's because it is so common that we tend not to take it very seriously. How many times have you told a friend to 'snap out of it' or 'don't be such a misery'? But depression, when it becomes extended, can be very serious and may affect our lives considerably.

What is depression?

What do we mean by depression? At its least serious it is simply a case of the 'blues', and we usually recover very quickly. Generally it is a feeling of unhappiness and helplessness – what Anthony Harris calls 'the loss of personal significance'. Reactive depression is directly related to stress, because it follows a particularly stressful circumstance – the death of a relative or long-term unemployment. Curing this sort of depression occurs either when the source of stress is removed or by helping the sufferer to come to terms with the problem.

The psychological response to stress arouses various emotions as a means of coping with a situation

Ask yourself

Line Manager

- Do I dismiss as irrelevant the emotional responses of my staff to the demands I make upon them?
- Do I encourage my staff to talk to me about how they feel about my demands?

Trainer

- Am I sensitive to the emotional climate in a group?
- Can I handle emotions effectively and positively?

Welfare Officer

- Do I regularly deal with clients who are suffering from depression?
- Have I attempted to correlate the spread of these clients with the demands of the workplace?

For all of us

- Do I try to suppress my emotions when faced with a difficult situation?
- Do I think that admitting to depression is a sign of weakness?

Your notes/personal points

Selected reading

BOOTH, A. L. *Stressmanship.* Chapter 13.

Anxiety

Anxiety can be induced by stress. When we talk about anxiety we usually mean that we have feelings of fear, misgivings and apprehension. Certain circumstances will make us feel anxious: starting a new job or meeting a group of strangers. Such feelings are perfectly healthy. We have them as a signal that there is a problem within us which we need to deal with, and mostly we recognise this and face up to our difficulty.

But anxiety can become much more serious. It can manifest itself as a feeling of uncontrolled panic. Our palms sweat, our hearts beat very fast and we become rooted to the spot. Often it may occur in a situation with which we are very familiar – travelling to work or in the local pub. There seems to be no reason for it. What has happened is that we have ignored the pressures which are on us at a conscious level, but our sub-conscious has remembered them so that it only takes a minor incident to push us into an anxiety attack. When this happens we must seek medical help and, in addition, identify the real stressors that have led to the attack and deal with them.

Change in behaviour

It is usually quite easy to recognise when people are undergoing a psychological response to stress because their behaviour changes. Sudden outbursts of temper, increasing irritability and procrastination are all indications that someone is finding their circumstances increasingly difficult to cope with. Conversely, some people react to stress by becoming more and more task-orientated, and rarely appear to relax. Others respond by absenteeism or an increase in minor sickness which keeps them away from work.

There may also be changes in someone's physical appearance. They may seem more strained and tense. Normally smart, they may begin to 'let themselves go'.

Where these signs are shown it is important that we take note of them as being a likely indication that the person is in difficulty, and try to find and remove the cause of the problem.

A change in behaviour can indicate that a person is suffering from stress

Ask yourself

Line Manager

- Do I dismiss changes in the behaviour of my staff as irrelevant to their work?
- Do I know everyone well enough to be aware when they are stressed?

Trainer

- Do I take into account that for many people a training event can cause anxiety?
- Am I aware of the stress effect upon myself of planning and running training events?

Welfare Officer

- Is it always possible to identify the cause of an individual's stress?
- Do I know enough about the working conditions of my clients to recognise the possible stressors?

For all of us

- Am I aware of any changes in my normal behaviour?
- Am I able to using coping techniques effectively to reduce stress?

Your notes/personal points

Selected reading

GOODWIN, R. *Stress at work.* Chapter 4.

Social response to stress

We live in a society in which we are constantly surrounded with 'props' to help us to cope with the pressures of modern life. Such props include tobacco, alcohol and tranquillizers. What they all have in common is that they distract our attention from the real problems. We become so used to them that we forget how to cope naturally. It is so much easier to pop a pill or have a drink than learn to relax.

Over-indulgence

As we become more stressed we have a tendency to turn to 'comfort tricks'. If something isn't going well then we comfort ourselves by buying a bar of chocolate or having a drink. The occasional use of a comfort trick can be beneficial. Where it becomes dangerous is when our 'comforter' becomes an intrinsic part of our life. The odd cigarette becomes 40 a day; the nip of whisky at the end of a long day turns into several; the valium we were prescribed in the short term becomes an addiction. And of course as we increase our use of cigarettes and alcohol we increase our stress because we know that we are doing ourselves harm.

Spicing up our lives

It also appears that when we are under stress we look for new experiences and tastes. So we may well experiment with exotic foods, which are hot and spicy, as a means of stimulating our tastebuds. We may look for more exciting drinks – perhaps that is why there has recently been an explosion in new spirits and liqueurs. Even more seriously we may turn to illegal drugs – heroin and cocaine. All of these are signs that we are refusing to recognise and deal with stress in our lives.

As we become stressed we tend to turn to artificial props to help us cope

Ask yourself

Line Manager

- Do any of my staff show a high degree of dependence on drink/cigarettes etc?
- What is my own view of alcoholism?

Trainer

- Do I keep an eye open for trainees who are resorting too heavily to comfort tricks?
- Am I clear in my own mind how to relay information about a trainee, whose behaviour is worrying, to the Line Manager or Welfare Officer?

Welfare Officer

- What is the rate of alcohol-related disease in my department?
- What positive steps should my department be taking to inform staff of the risks of alcohol, tobacco and drug abuse?

For all of us

- Am I placing too much reliance on a 'prop'?
- What is my favourite comfort trick?

_____

Your notes/personal points

_____

Selected reading

CHAITOW, L. *Your complete stress-proofing programme.*

Stress and our health

By now it seems clear that there is a definite link between stress and our health. This link manifests itself in many ways:

- our body's automatic reaction to stress releases hormones which contribute to serious ill-health
- our body's reactions to stress lessen the ability of our immune systems to cope with disease
- dealing with stress inappropriately causes our personal relationships to alter and makes it harder for us to face reality
- dealing with stress by using props such as alcohol can in itself increase the likelihood of disease

Dealing sensibly with stress

We have looked in some detail at the different signs which can give us clues that we are probably heading for a danger level of stress in our lives, and at the illnesses that can result if we ignore these signs. On the next pages you will find a chart summarising them, and then some questionnaires which will help you to assess your own health in relation to stress. It is important to realise that exhibiting symptoms of stress does not necessarily mean that you are heading for dangerous health problems. There are other factors such as age, diet and exercise which play a part. Everybody has a different

Ask yourself

For all of us

- Is my life style and diet as sensible and appropriate as it ought to be?
- Do I recognise in myself any of the symptoms on the opposite page?

Note Try the questionnaires on page 34 for yourself, or if appropriate, with members of your staff or with trainees.

tolerance level. Nevertheless these are signs which our bodies exhibit to act as a warning to us. It is only sensible to heed that warning.

Symptoms which can indicate stress

PHYSICAL	<ul><li>losing sleep</li><li>headaches</li><li>impotence</li><li>muscle tension</li><li>minor illnesses</li></ul>
PSYCHOLOGICAL/ EMOTIONAL/ BEHAVIOURAL	<ul><li>difficulty concentrating</li><li>lack of self-worth</li><li>more pessimistic and unhappy</li><li>increased anxiety</li><li>feeling tense and strained</li><li>irritability</li><li>indecision</li><li>absenteeism</li></ul>
SOCIAL	<ul><li>increased use of stimulants: tobacco alcohol food drugs</li></ul>

There is a link between stress in our lives and personal health

Your notes/personal points

Selected reading

EDMUNDS, L. 'How to look for tell-tale signs of stress.' *Daily Telegraph.* 3 February 1984. p 17.

Questionnaire: Am I suffering from the emotional effects of stress?

Tick the answer that most applies to you.
OFTEN   – More than once a week
SOMETIMES   – More than once a month
RARELY   – Less than once a month

	Often	Some	Rare
Do I ever feel unable to cope?			
Do I find it difficult to relax?			
Do I ever feel anxious for no reason?			
Do I find it hard to show my true feelings?			
Am I finding it hard to make decisions?			
Am I often irritable for no real reason?			
Do I worry about the future?			
Do I feel isolated and misunderstood?			
Do I like myself?			
Am I finding it hard to concentrate?			
Am I worried about my health?			
Do I find that life has lost its sparkle?			

Scoring Score one for every answer you have ticked in the 'OFTEN' box.

A score of 0– 3	indicates slight stress
A score of 4– 6	indicates moderate stress
A score of 7–11	indicates severe stress
A score of 12	indicates very severe stress – you should seek medical help

If you scored more than 3 then it indicates that your body is trying to adapt to stress. See these signs as a warning and take some action to reduce those things in your life which are causing you stress. Other parts of this book will give you some ideas of how you can do this. Try this questionnaire again in a few months and see if there is any improvement.

Questionnaire: Am I suffering from the physical effects of stress?

Tick the answer that most applies to you.
OFTEN   – More than once a week
SOMETIMES   – More than once a month
RARELY   – Less than once a month

	Often	Some	Rare
Do I ever have aching shoulders or neck muscles?			
Do I have trouble sleeping?			
Do I have persistent indigestion?			
Am I feeling unusually tired?			
Do I have frequent headaches?			
Is my blood pressure too high?			
Do I have unexplained dizzy spells?			
Do I smoke to calm my nerves?			
Do I eat erratically?			
Do I ever feel nauseous?			
Do I have a drink to unwind?			
Am I experiencing sexual difficulties?			
Do I have unexplained skin rashes?			

Scoring Score one for every answer you have ticked in the 'OFTEN' box.

A score of 0– 3	indicates slight stress
A score of 4– 6	indicates moderate stress
A score of 7–11	indicates severe stress
A score of 12–plus	indicates very severe stress – you should seek medical help

If you scored more than 3 then it indicates that your body is trying to adapt to stress. See these signs as a warning and take some action to reduce those things in your life that are causing you stress. Section 4, 'Management and coping skills', will give you some ideas of how you can do this. Try this questionnaire again in a few months and see if there is any improvement.

Stress and work performance

All of us at some time or other have probably felt stressed about our work: coming home after a particularly hard day; or when we have to meet a deadline. Situations like these can make us feel irritable and over-tired.

Sometimes we find that stress can be helpful. It acts as a motivator and keeps us going for a short period. Work stress should never be a permanent feature of our lives. We do not need to operate at top pressure all the time to produce good work, even though we may feel sometimes that if we slow down then we will not be able to cope. Very many people have a high level of job satisfaction, produce good work and are not envincing symptoms of stress. If they can do it, so can we all.

The human resource

People are usually the most costly element of any organization's budget. Often though we seem to be more concerned with maintaining machinery and equipment than keeping our workforce healthy and functioning on all four cylinders! If we look back at some of the symptoms of stress we can see that most of them are likely to impair work performance:

- **Stress can be DANGEROUS** – lack of concentration can cause accidents

- **Stress can be COSTLY** – indecision may lose us an important contract. Key people may have to leave because of ill-health

- **Stress can be DAMAGING** – irritability may give our organization a poor public image

The list goes on. You can probably add more examples of how stress can diminish work performance. Overall we can say that

Negative stress = Inefficiency

Recognizing stress at work

In 1977, MORI conducted a poll which found that 12 per cent of the workforce had been off work during the last year with mental strain. Millions of working days are lost each year due to minor illnesses – backache, stomach disorders, headaches. It makes sense to ask ourselves if we, or our staff, are suffering unduly from work stress, and to monitor stress levels. Everyone will benefit.

Stress at work is costly and leads to inefficiency and loss of personal job satisfaction

Ask yourself

Line Manager

- Is there any change in the pattern of accidents or dangerous incidents at work?

- Does anyone seem to have difficulty concentrating?

Trainer

- Do any of my trainees seem to have undue difficulty in concentrating?

- How can I harness potential stress to make my training events more interesting and effective?

Welfare Officer

- How does the pattern of reported work accidents and incidents in my department compare with other departments or the organization as a whole?

- Have there been more complaints from the public or other departments recently than are normally received?

For all of us

- Does the way my work is organized currently cause periods of greater stress?

- Could I, either alone or with co-operation, reorganize/rearrange my work pattern so that it is less stressful?

Your notes/personal points

Selected reading

MARSHALL, J. and COOPER, C. L. (ed.) *Coping with stress at work: Case studies from industry.* Chapter 4.

Questionnaire: Work performance

You might find it useful to ask your staff to complete the following questionnaire. If it is used together with the questionnaires about the EMOTIONAL EFFECTS and PHYSICAL EFFECTS of stress you will have a very clear idea of where trouble is likely to occur.

If you find that either you, or the people with whom you work, are showing signs of unacceptable stress levels then it will be worthwhile talking about why, and looking for solutions to reduce stress levels. You can find out more about causes of work stress in Section 3 of this book.

Do this questionnaire and find out your stress score. The situations listed are fairly typical which everyone meets from time to time, and they should be taken in one's stride. However if they occur frequently, you will have to take active steps to reduce their number, or improve your overall balance of health, and develop support groups outside your work to enable you to cope with them. On the right you will see how often they occur: never, rarely, sometimes, often and always. After each sentence ring the score that applies to you, and then add up your total.

How do you score?

0 – 20 The stressors are about average for most people who enjoy their work but inevitably find things frustrating from time to time.

21–45 The stressors are such that you get tense and uptight from time to time and you will have to follow the relaxation techniques.

45+ The stressors are too high. Are you perhaps a Type 'A' personality, a worrier or a perfectionist?

	NEVER	RARELY	SOMETIMES	OFTEN	ALWAYS
I cannot get my work finished in time.	1	2	3	4	5
I haven't the time to do things as I would like them to be done.	1	2	3	4	5
I'm not clear exactly what my responsibilities are.	1	2	3	4	5
I haven't enough to occupy my mind or my time.	1	2	3	4	5
I don't get on with my boss.	1	2	3	4	5
I lack confidence in dealing with people.	1	2	3	4	5
I have unsettled conflicts with other staff.	1	2	3	4	5
I get very little support from my colleagues or my superiors.	1	2	3	4	5
I never know how I'm getting on in my job. There's no feedback.	1	2	3	4	5
No one understands the needs of my department.	1	2	3	4	5
Our targets/budgets are unrealistic and unworkable.	1	2	3	4	5
I have to take work home to get it done.	1	2	3	4	5
I have to work at weekends to get everything done.	1	2	3	4	5
I can never take all my leave.	1	2	3	4	5
I avoid any difficult situations.	1	2	3	4	5
I feel frustrated.	1	2	3	4	5

Total Score_____

Section 3.
Causes of stress

Contents

Using this section

This section can be used in two ways:

- If you are new to the subject of stress you will find it helpful to read through the whole section.
- On the other hand you will find it useful to dip into this section as a reminder. For example, you may want to use one of the questionnaires for yourself or with colleagues.

To help you dip into, or skim read, the material, each topic has a clear heading and the **Key point** is picked out in bold type.

By the time you have completed this section you will be able to:

- define some of the factors which can cause stress
- understand why the incidence of stress is high in the 20th century
- differentiate between personal and organizational stresses
- begin to identify those stressors which affect you personally

Where appropriate, reading relevant to the subject matter is listed for your information.

Introduction

Having defined stress and looked at the symptoms associated with extreme reactions to stress, we now turn to examining some potential causes or stressors.

The list of potential stressors is enormous. Indeed it might be argued that almost anything in life has the potential to produce a stress reaction because it demands an adjustment. Some stressors of course are common and will affect all of us. Examples are extremes of temperature, lack of food, sleep deprivation etc. But other stressors are much more personal and our reactions to them will depend very largely on our genetic and environmental make-up.

In this section therefore it is important to remember that not all the stressors identified will necessarily be stress-inducing to all individuals. They should be seen as a guide to help you rather than as a definitive listing. There may also be certain events which you think should have been included and which do not appear — note these in the spaces provided.

We do know, from research with many groups, that there appear to be certain common events in people's lives which have the capacity to cause distress. In this section you will find a 'Life Events Inventory' which you can use to assess your personal stress level.

Finally, as we have already said, it is important to remember that stressful events can be potentially useful in giving us that little bit of extra lift to get us through difficult situations. It is only when the exposure to that event is maintained over a long period that our ability to adapt is strained and we are liable to cause ourselves damage.

The final section of this book deals with how to manage stress and describes certain methods of coping with stress which you may find useful.

Stress and society

Why is it that the effects of stress and particularly stress-related disease are perceived as a 20th century phenomenon? The use of the word 'stress' has existed since the 14th century, but it is difficult to find its modern association before the mid-19th century. It is then that a French physiologist, Claude Bernard, suggested that environmental changes can have an effect on organisms – the first recognition of the importance of keeping a balance between the body and the environment. But can we deduce from this, therefore, that before the present there was no such thing as a stressed person?

Stress and early peoples

If we recall that the stress response is an automatic reaction of the body to danger, it follows that there must always have been stressors in our lives. Early peoples were provided with the 'fight or flight' response to get them out of danger from natural predators. As they evolved from the role of 'hunter-gatherers' so the qualities necessary for survival changed. People no longer needed the reaction to remove themselves from predators. What they required were qualities to enable them to survive in settlements interacting with others. But instead of slowly evolving into this new way of life people suddenly had to adapt to a social environment which imposed new and alien stressors.

The new predators

As civilisation extended its boundaries, large towns and cities grew up very quickly in evolutionary terms. People were faced not with the tigers of the past but new predators in the form of role conflict, work conflict, noise and pollution. The lean and powerful hunting mammal was no longer required. Instead the new leaders were revered for their mental rather than their physical qualities. In these circumstances it is hardly surprising that the concept of stress and stress-related illness begins to come to the fore. Stress as a response is not new – but the pressures of urban life are.

The concept of stress and stress-related disease is attributable to the rapid changes in our environment

Ask yourself

Line Manager

- Do you too easily dismiss stress as unimportant?
- Do you believe that only managers suffer from stress?

Trainer

- Do you understand the subject matter well enough to talk about it?
- Can you marshall arguments and evidence to suit different training and information events?

Welfare Officer

- Have you considered whether some of the problems brought to you may be stress-induced?

Your notes/personal points

Selected reading

HARRIS, A. B. *Breakpoint: Stress and the crisis of modern living.* Chapter 1.

The effects of the 20th century

Before the Industrial Revolution we lived in a relatively stable society. Change tended to take place over centuries rather than months. People had defined roles and 'knew their place'. Opportunities for mobility in terms of both physical location and status were limited. Women were expected to undertake the role of carer; men were expected to provide for the family. All this, of course is a gross-oversimplification, but is nevertheless true in broad emphasis. All this changed with the advent of the technological and social advances of the Industrial Revolution. In a comparatively short period the 'old order' disappeared. Suddenly, people were forced to adapt from a predominantly agricultural economy to one based on manufacturing. Enormous industrial conurbations sprang up. 'Trade' became respectable. Work patterns changed and roles within the family altered.

The 'new order'

As technology increased so did the *pace* of change. Noise, speed, pollution, overcrowding are stressors which are very recent in our lives. We have not been able to evolve to cope with them – they have been thrust upon us. Achievement and status are the new gods which we are constantly exhorted to worship. Nowadays 'anyone can become President' we are told – what we often forget is that not everybody wants to be.

The results

If we accept that stress is a response made by our bodies to demands it is clear that the 20th century has produced a *sudden and increasing* series of demands, with the inevitable consequences that this has for our physical and mental health. We have not had the time to evolve to adapt – the changes are coming at us too thick and fast. So we must find new skills to mitigate the effect of those demands and help us to cope.

It is the pace of change which has led to the concept of stress as a 20th century phenomenon

Ask yourself

Line Manager

- How much do I know about my staff outside the work relationship?
- Does it matter?

Trainer

- Am I sufficiently up-to-date with the social conditions and life styles experienced by my potential trainees?
- Do the social stresses to which I am subjected affect my own efficiency or objectivity?

Welfare Officer

- How can I work to minimise the effects of social stress?
- Should I concern myself only with reactive strategies?

For all of us

- Am I aware of changes or increases in the demands made on me?

Your notes/personal points

Selected reading

BOOTH, A. L. *Stressmanship.* pp 48–49.

Technological change

The world that most of us live in today is very different from even when we were children. Many of us can easily recall the introduction of television, the first mainframe computer, the atomic bomb, Concorde, nuclear power. The list of changes in technology over the last forty years is endless, and we can all give examples of things which we now use everyday which, only a short while ago, were unknown. Suddenly the world is the province of the young – remember the 'golden hellos' of the computer whizz-kids when the city of London was preparing for the 'Big Bang'? Yet most of us were brought up to regard our elders with veneration for their experience. We looked to them for knowledge – now we look to the young.

Accelerated change

Coupled with this shifting of values, the *rate* of technological change has increased out of all proportion. A cursory glance at the pages of any newspaper reveals almost daily new discoveries and inventions. Alvin Toffler in his book *Future shock* graphically described the acceleration of the rate of change. He pointed out that over the last 50,000 years of our existence or 800 generations it is only in the last two that we have been able to accurately measure time and have the power of electricity at our disposal. It is only in this present generation, he adds, that 'the overwhelming majority of all the material goods that we use today have been developed'.

Physical wealth/psychological ill-health

It is true that most of us live today in circumstances that are greatly improved. We have more material possessions and we have greater expectations. This very improvement has introduced new and important stressors into our lives:

- the rate of change which demands a rate of adaptation, which we cannot produce

- an expectation of material wealth, which may not be met.

Technology itself has been responsible for reducing as well as increasing living standards when it has led to changes in work and social patterns.

Thus technology is a double-edged sword, and we should be aware of its potential for causing distress in our lives.

Technological change may provide us with physical wealth and psychological ill-health

Ask yourself

Line Manager

- What other motivation factors can I use besides pay and conditions?

- Can I decrease pressure on people by better use of flexitime or alternative working patterns?

Trainer

- Does the increasing use of technology in training bother me?

- Can I cope with 'technofear' in my trainees?

Welfare Officer

- Do I try to forecast the effect of change?

For all of us

- Am I too hooked on wealth and the aquisition of possessions? Why?

Your notes/personal points

Selected reading
NORFOLK, D. *Executive stress.* Chapter 4.

The decline of the extended family

What does the word 'family' conjure up for you? Most likely it brings to mind a vision of two parents and their two children. It's unlikely that your mental picture included aunts, uncles, cousins and grandparents. And yet, not so many years ago, the family was not the precise and closed unit which we tend to think of today. People lived in small communities, and a house often had several generations living together.

Support systems

The modern concept of the family is rather restricted and, very importantly, it has taken away from all of us a support structure. By a support structure we mean a system of relationships which interacts to care for each individual within it. Nowadays, with increased mobility it is not uncommon for the extended family to be scattered all over the country, if not all over the world. We are left isolated and do not have the same care network that what was once an integral part of our lives.

The nuclear family

At the same time as the extended family has declined, so the concept of the nuclear family has grown up. Perhaps this is best exemplified by the sorts of the families we see on TV advertisements: working father, homemaker mother and two freshly scrubbed children. So often are we assailed with this image that it comes as a shock to realise that this sort of family is actually a minority in modern life! Sixty-five per cent of households have no children. Four per cent are single parent families. Sixteen per cent have both parents working. Only 13 per cent of households have the 'typical' image which is so carefully nurtured by the media, adding additional stressors by making us feel guilty for not conforming to what most of us believe to be the norm.

The decline of the extended family and the media stereotyping of the nuclear family have added additional stressors to our lives

Ask yourself

Line Manager

- Do I expect my staff to leave their family problems at home?
- Do I try to be a 'superperson'?

Trainer

- How do I challenge my trainee's assumptions and media stereotyping?
- How do I challenge *my own*

Welfare Officer

- Am I always aware of the home circumstances of my clients?
- Do I have any unconscious prejudices about how people ought to balance home and work pressures?

For all of us

- How can I improve my support system?

Your notes/personal points

Selected reading

KING, J. and STOTT, M. (ed.) *Is this your life?* pp 37–64.

Loneliness

From the moment we are born most of us are brought up to expect to spend our lives in interaction with other people. We go to schools, we join churches and social clubs. We work with others. Opportunities for travel to visit friends and relatives have never been easier. Given all the multitudinous ways of making social contact it would seem that, whatever else may be a stressor in the 20th century, loneliness can be discounted. If that is the case, why then are the 'problem pages' in magazines full of letters from people expressing their loneliness?

A 'cog in the machine'

Perhaps the best way of understanding the phenomenon of loneliness is to equate it with personal significance. It is a sad, but inevitable fact of life, that many of us have become reduced to ciphers. We travel to work with millions of others. We carry out tasks repeated by millions of others. We live in homes which are repeated in their thousands throughout the country. To take one particular example, unemployment is no longer a personal tragedy – we are merely part of the unemployment statistics. We can all cite examples of bad planning which has resulted in people becoming more and more cut off from the communities of the past. Ironically, technology has increased the opportunity to extend our social relationships – and at the same time has changed the nature of personal relationships, for example TV has largely replaced conversation. Loneliness doesn't mean you are alone – one can be lonely among other people.

Physical and social needs

Unlike the physical needs which we all have – eating to survive, for example — the need to interact with others is one which is instilled into us from birth. But, just as depriving us of food is damaging, depriving ourselves of company can be equally damaging. We need other people to provide us with a sense of esteem and social worth.

Loneliness is a powerful social stressor

Ask yourself

Line Manager

- Do I accept that I have a responsibility for my staff's welfare?
- Do I talk *with* them or *at* them?

Trainer

- Am I aware of the value of interpersonal skills training?
- How important is interpersonal skill for me?

Welfare Officer

- Do I understand the problems of loneliness and isolation?
- Is my liaison with Line Managers and Trainers sufficiently strong to create the relevant support?

For all of us

- Do I have friends or just acquaintances?
- Am I willing to discuss problems with my friends and family?

Your notes/personal points

Selected reading

BOOTH, A. L. *Stressmanship.* Chapter 3.

Personal relationships

We have already said something of the potentially stressful effects of the decline of the extended family and loneliness. Both of these are tied in with the way in which we relate to other people – our social skills.

How successful we are in our lives – success in terms of leading a fulfilling and meaningful life – depends on how well we are able to interact with others. To interact successfully we require certain skills: communication, listening, responding – these are all skills which we have to learn.

Faulty social skills

If we are deficient in our skills in dealing with other people then this can be very stressful. Faulty skills mean that we will have difficulty in relating well to others and in adapting to our social circumstances. To take an extreme example, someone who goes to prison for the first time may well find that they have to learn an entirely new set of responses if they are to survive in their new environment. Personal relationships which are in a constant state of friction mean that we miss out on the rewards of friendship and love – not deliberately, but simply because we do not know how to adjust.

Effects of poor relationships

If our social skills are undeveloped then we find that many of our needs for security and affection are unfulfilled. We became isolated and our thinking becomes disordered because we don't have other people to talk things through with us. As we become isolated so we become frustrated and bitter about other people. We become depressed and alienated. It is a vicious circle: the worse our skills in dealing with people, the more likely is it we will lose contact. The more we lose contact the worse our skills become. And so it goes on. If we recognise that our social skills are not as well developed as they might be, then it makes sense to try and redress the balance – often training can be helpful in this area.

Poorly developed social skills become a source of personal stress by leading us to feel alienated from our society

Ask yourself

Line Manager

- Do I encourage my staff to discuss problems with me?
- Do I listen?

Trainer

- Do I need to revise/update my approach to social skills training?
- Do I use my own social skills effectively in my work?

Welfare Officer

- Do I liaise/work with Line Managers and Trainers closely enough?
- Do I see my clients as 'people' as well as 'cases'?

For all of us

- Do I bottle things up too much?

Your notes/personal points

Selected reading
BLAUG, P. M. 'Social exchange' in *Sociological Perspectives:* Selected reading edited by THOMPSON, K. and TUNSTALL, J. pp 220–233.

Community status

As we have seen, life in the 20th century introduces a multitude of new stressors to our lives. One stressor that is as old as the hills and yet takes on a new meaning in modern society is that of status. Since time immemorial people have tended to bestow approval according to how they perceive others in society as a whole. Thus the pecking order, or hierarchy, of which we are all familiar. The old nursery rhyme 'I'm the king of the castle, and you're the dirty rascal' puts this nicely into context for us.

Does status matter?

Status, or rather perception of status, becomes important as a force in our lives when there is a misfit between what our expectations are and what our actual experience is. If the two coincide then there is unlikely to be any stressful effect. When there is a misfit the result is conflict between what we want and what we have. 'Keeping up with the Jones's' is a familiar phrase which seems in these consumerist days to have become a maxim for all of us. Nowadays the Jones's aren't just the family down the street – they are the images with which we are constantly surrounded on television, in advertising and in the printed media. Thus our expectations take on a more frenzied and less attainable character – and hence become a new stressor in our lives. It isn't status that matters – it is our expectations of status.

Our place in the hierarchy

Sometimes, of course, our real status can be a stressor in itself. If we are fairly low down in the scheme of things then we probably find ourselves facing difficulties associated with that position. We may earn less. We lack power. We lack control over our own lives, and other people, our bosses for example, are able to discipline us. This can be particularly difficult if our expectations are much higher. For example, the skilled craftsperson whose skills are no longer required can find it very difficult to adjust to a work environment where those skills are not used.

Both our perceived and our real status in society can act as stressors

Ask yourself

Line Manager

- Am I overly concerned with maintaining my own status?
- Do I take positive steps to maximize the potential of my staff or do I find this threatening?

Trainer

- How restricted am I as a trainer by my place in the hierarchy?
- Am I concerned with 'delivering' information or encouraging people to *learn*?
- Am I affected by the position in the hierarchy of my students?

Welfare Officer

- Does my perceived status limit my effectiveness?
- Am I willing to challenge other people's perception of status if necessary?

For all of us

- How important to me is keeping up with the Jones'?

Your notes/personal points

Selected reading

HOWARD, R. W. *Coping and adapting: How you can learn to cope with stress.* pp 32–35.

Unemployment/retirement

'Work is a grand cure for all the maladies and miseries that ever beset mankind.'*

We live in a society that practices what is sometimes called the 'Protestant work ethic', that is, a society that values a person by their work contribution. Given this innate belief it is hardly surprising that unemployment is an enormous stressor in itself. People who retire or become unemployed may tend after the initial shock to experience a feeling of euphoria – because they have got away from the stressors in the workplace. But this may quickly be replaced with feelings of helplessness and despair. As the length of unemployment or time away from work increases so too do the stressors associated with unemployment or retirement.

Associated stressors

It is not just the fact of not having a job which makes unemployment such a powerful stressor. The results of that unemployment or retirement also contribute. These results could include: a lower standard of living (so that life becomes a constant struggle to meet the next bill); a lowering of self-worth; an increased sense of fatalism; more leisure time but less ability to fill that time; lack of contact with others through not being able to afford to go out. All of these are additional stressors to the major stressor of not having paid work.

Is work necessary?

Selye states that 'work is a biological necessity' and says that we all need to find 'the occupation which to us is play'. However much we may disagree or agree with Selye, there is no doubt that, because of the expectations of society, unemployment can cause great personal distress. A dichotomy is created between what what we believe to be our right and our actual experience.

Unemployment and retirement are stressors, each with additional associated stressors

---

*Thomas Carlyle, *Inaugural address,* Edinburgh, 2 April 1866.

Ask yourself

Line Manager

- Can I help my staff prepare for retirement?

Trainer

- How can training prepare people for retirement?

Welfare Officer

- What steps can I encourage the organization to take to prepare people for retirement?

For all of us

- Am I my work?

Your notes/personal points

Selected reading

SELYE, H. *Stress without distress.* pp 82–92.

Bereavement and loss

The death of a spouse is generally agreed to be the most stressful event that we can experience. Of course death, expected or unexpected, will inevitably cause us to feel pain and loss. Perhaps though in the twentieth century it has taken on a new and more profound significance. An old proverb says 'the first breath is the beginning of death' – which emphasises that the only truth we know about life is that we will all die. Death is a natural process, but in this age it is still one of the last taboo subjects. We rarely discuss death, we have all sorts of euphemisms, for example 'passed away' – it is a concept with which most of us are very uncomfortable.

Expectation of life and fear of death

Sometimes the fear of death becomes an obsession. Accepting that death is a reality and then getting on with the business of life is the only way to cope. Grieving has its part to play in helping with the coping.

The loss cycle

Bereavement and other great losses, your home or your job for example, trigger off a stress reaction. It begins with a period of extreme grief which may be followed by a denial that the loss has occurred. Feelings of guilt, 'It should have been me' and anger 'How could they let this happen?', are common. Finally comes the stage of acceptance and the resolve to continue. This is all perfectly normal. Unfortunately, some people are unable to progress through the cycle. Either they can't grieve or they never reach the stage of acceptance. The loss becomes a permanent source of stress in their life. Such people will need professional counselling to work through their feelings and come to terms with their loss. Without help it is possible that they might give up to the pressure of their loss and, ultimately, die. This is the phenomenon called 'the mortality of bereavement'.

It is normal to have a stress reaction to death and loss, but an over or under reaction may become a permanent and debilitating stressor

Ask yourself

Line Manager

- Do I understand how devastating bereavement can be?
- Do I appreciate that reaction to bereavement can be long term?

Welfare Officer

- Do I encourage the bereaved to express grief?
- Am I aware that other losses, besides death, can provoke a reaction similar to bereavement?

For all of us

- Am I obsessed with death?

  Who can I discuss my fears with?

Your notes/personal points

Selected reading

PARKES, C. M. *Bereavement: Studies of grief in adult life.* Chapter 3.

You and your self image

By now it should be clear that changes in your environment may well provoke a stress reaction. How well you cope with the changes will depend on factors within you, your genes and your heredity. The combination of these factors contribute to your self image – the way you perceive yourself to be. Having a *positive* self image can be a vital ingredient in your response to change and your reaction to stressors.

Self-fulfilling prophecies

From a very early age we are brought up to expect that certain things are inevitable in our lives. Marriage is a good example of this. The way our parents react can also be crucial. If we are constantly told that we are very clever or very stupid then eventually we may begin to accept these opinions as truths. By doing so we end up expecting too much or too little, and our self-image is distorted. We have all come across the person who is always asking for love and affection; we have also all met the person who seems to expect that their life will be unpleasant and unfulfilling.

Know yourself

Our views of ourselves are often distorted by our experiences and expectations. We may not be aware that we are holding irrational beliefs because we have such difficulty in perceiving reality. But knowing yourself and your abilities is a prerequisite for handling stress. Try writing down ten statements beginning with the words 'I am......' then discuss them with someone you trust. You may be surprised at how different, and much more positive, their view is from yours. When something happens to us, however trivial, which is at odds with our self belief then its stress effect may be enormous.

Self image is an important factor in our reaction to stressors

Ask yourself

You and your environment

So far in this section we have looked at some of the facets of modern life which help to explain why stress is sometimes called the scourge of the twentieth century. Some of us will recognise these as being particularly important in explaining stress in our own lives. Others of us will not find these potential stressors playing much of a role. Nevertheless, there is a case for examining our own environments to try and isolate anything which may be a cause of stress. Following next is a 'Life Events Inventory' to assess the level of stressful occurrences in your life. Before we reach that stage however, you may find it helpful to spend a few minutes thinking about yourself and your role in society.

- What do you like about the world you live in?
- What about it makes you unhappy?
- Are there any changes you can make which would improve things?
- Are you conscious of loneliness?
- Does change distress you?
- Have you expectations which haven't been fulfilled?
- How do you react to people who do not 'conform'?
- Do you have problems with your personal relationships, either at home or at work?

You may have found that thinking about these questions has identified some potential stressors in your life which you weren't aware of. If that is the case try to talk about your feelings with a close friend or someone else you trust. You may also find it helpful to read Section 4, Managing stress, in this book.

Life Events Inventory*

Which of the following events have happened to you in the past 12 months?

Events	Scale value
Death of spouse	100
Divorce	73
Marital separation	65
Imprisonment	63
Death of close family member	63
Personal injury or illness	53
Marriage	50
Dismissal from work	47
Marital reconciliation	45
Retirement	45
Change in health of family member	44
Pregnancy	40
Sex difficulties	39
Gain of new family member	39
Business readjustment	39
Change in financial state	38
Change in number of arguments with spouse	35
Major mortgage or loan	32
Foreclosure of mortgage or loan	30
Change in responsibilities at work	29
Children leaving home	29
Trouble with in-laws	29
Outstanding personal achievement	28
Partner begins or stops work	26
Begin or end of school or college	26
Change in living conditions	25
Change of personal habits	24
Trouble with boss	23
Change in work hours or conditions	20
Change in residence	20
Change in schools or college	20
Change in recreation	19
Change in church activities	19
Change in social activities	18
Minor mortgage or loan	17
Change in sleeping habits	16
Change in number of family meetings	15
Change in eating habits	15
Vacation	13
Christmas	12
Minor violations of the law	11

Add together the total number of points to obtain your stress potential and then read the notes that follow.

*Taken from HOLMES, T. H. and RAHE, R. H. 'The social readjustment rating scale' in *Journal of Psychosomatic Research*: 1967.

The life events inventory

The inventory that you have just completed was designed by two researchers into life changes and stress. Holmes and Rahe devised the list and tested it with a great many people from different backgrounds and cultures.

The inventory is based on the idea that changes in your life cause stress and that some changes cause more stress than others.

Holmes and Rahe found that:

150–199 points increase your likelihood of illness by 40 per cent

200–299 points increase your likelihood of illness by 50 per cent

300 points and over increase your likelihood of illness by 80 per cent

Don't worry too much if your score seems to be very high. Other factors, like your personality and how well you react to change have to be taken into account also. If you're the sort of person who positively welcomes change then you will probably fall into the percentage of those who will be alright.

Also, of course some events might actually remove stress – a divorce for example might be preferable to the pain of living in a relationship which is causing personal friction.

You may also find this scale useful as a gauge for measuring what your life in the next 12 months will be like in terms of stress. If you know that you will be moving house, planning a family, and taking on a large mortgage then it would make sense to try and space out any other changes – like taking on a new job – until you have got through the other changes.

Who suffers from stress at work?

The typical reaction of most people when asked this question is to reply that it is a problem experienced by managers, that is, the more responsibility and authority a person has, the more likely they are to be overstressed.

While there is evidence to show that managers identify their work as a source of stress in general it appears that this has a positive rather than negative effect. This is because people in managerial and executive positions are better able to cope because of their expectations – that is, they expect and enjoy the demands placed upon them. American actuarial studies confirm this by showing that the death rate among company presidents is only 58 per cent of the average for the country's white males.

What about non-managers?

Interestingly, it seems that, contrary to popular belief, people who occupy work with a high degree of responsibility but a low degree of authority are much more likely to suffer from the effects of stress. Some of the particular aspects of non-managerial work which are most responsible for stress include:

- a lack of control or involvement
- insufficient mental stimulation
- high noise levels
- repetitive and dull tasks

So it is not necessarily the *number* of demands but the *acceptability* of those demands which is the key factor in determining who is likely to suffer from stress at work.

People at the top of the hierarchy tend to suffer less stress than those at the bottom

Ask yourself

Line Manager

- Do I understand how work stressors affect my staff?
- Do I accept that adverse stress affects everyone?

Trainer

- Do I ever raise unrealistic expectations by my training?
- What can I do to help people cope better with the stressors present in their work?

Welfare Officer

- Can I collaborate more effectively with line managers to reduce the effect of work stressors?

For all of us

- Am I aware of those factors in my occupation which cause me most stress?

Your notes/personal points

Selected reading

ZALEZNIK, A. et al. 'Stress reactions in organizations' in *Behavioural Science*. Vol. 22, No. 3, May 1977. pp 151–162.

Are particular jobs more prone to stress?

The type of work that people do has a relationship with stress. Generally the most stressful jobs are those which have a responsibility for people – such as the police, teaching, nursing, and personnel. The possibility of physical danger – either to oneself or to others also plays a part. The table below is the result of research into stress factors in a range of occupations. Organizations which want to detect if particular jobs are stress-prone should draw up their own tables using their medical records.

Occupational stress ratings: Stress increases with numbers on 0–10 scale

Financial areas

Accountancy	4·3
Banking	3·7
Building societies	3·3
Insurance	3·8
Actuary	3·3
Stockbroker	5·5
Average	4·0

Commerce/management

Advertising	7·3
Management	5·8
Marketing/export	5·8
Market research	4·3
Personnel	6·0
Public relations	5·8
Purchasing and supply	4·5
Sales and retailing	5·7
Secretary	4·7
Company secretary	5·3
Work study/O & M	3·6
Average	5·3

Arts and communications

Art and design	4·2
Broadcasting	6·8
Journalism	7·5
Museums	2·8
Photographer	4·6
Publishing	5·0
Musician	6·3
Actor	7·2
Film production	6·5
Professional sport (footballer, etc)	5·8
Librarian	2·0
Average	5·3

Health

Chiropodist	4·0
Dentistry	7·3
Dietetics	3·4
Environmental health	4·6
Doctor	6·8
Nursing/midwifery	6·5
Occupational therapy	3·7
Optician	4·0
Osteopath	4·3
Pharmacist	4·5
Vets	4·5
Physiotherapy	4·2
Radiographer	4·0
Remedial gymnast	3·5
Speech therapy	4·0
Average	4·6

Environment

Farming	4·8
Forestry	4·8
Horticulture	3·8
Nature conservancy	3·2
Average	4·2

Public administration

Civil Service	4·4
Diplomatic Service	4·8
Local government officer	4·3
Town and Country Planning	4·0
Sports/recreation admin	3·5
Average	4·2

Uniformed professions

Armed forces	4·7
Pilot (civil aviation)	7·5
Merchant Navy	4·8
Fireman	6·3
Police	7·7
Prison officer	7·5
Ambulance service	6·3
Average	6·4

Caring professions

Nursery nurse	3·3
Social worker	6·0
Teacher	6·2
Youth and community work	4·2
Church	3·5
Psychologist	5·2
Average	4·7

Professional services	
Architecture	4·0
Barrister	5·7
Solicitor	4·3
Surveyor	4·3
Estate agent	4·3
	——
Average	4·4

Technical specialities	
Biologist	3·0
Chemist	3·7
Computer	3·8
Engineer	4·3
Geologist	3·7
Lab technician	3·8
Metallurgist	3·8
Operational research	3·8
Packaging	3·8
Patent work	4·2
Physicist	3·4
Biochemist	3·6
Statistician	4·0
Linguist	3·6
Astronomer	3·4
	——
Average	3·7

Personal service industries	
Catering/hotels, etc	5·3
Travel	4·8
Hairdresser	4·3
Beauty therapy	3·5
	——
Average	4·5

Public service industries	
Post and telecommunications	4·0
Gas	4·0
Electricity	4·6
Water	4·0
Public transport	5·4
	——
Average	4·5

Industrial production	
Ceramic technology	4·0
Food technology	4·0
Printing	5·6
Plastic and rubber	4·5
Textiles/clothing technology	4·5
Timber/furniture technology	4·3
Leather/footwear technology	3·8
Mining	8·3
Construction/building	7·5
Brewing	4·0
	——
Average	5·1

Average rates	
6·4	Uniformed professions
5·3	Commerce/management
5·3	Arts/communications
5·1	Industrial production
4·7	Caring professions
4·6	Health
4·5	Personal services
4·5	Public services
4·4	Professional services
4·2	Environment
4·2	Public administration
4·0	Financial areas
3·7	Technical specialities

Source: University of Manchester Institute of Science and Technology

Individuals in organizations

Overall we can summarise by saying that it is the *fit* between the expectations of the individual, the organization and the work which is important. Within each of these three areas there are stimuli which can cause stress. If there is conflict between the stimuli and the overall fit then stress will result. The table that follows illustrates this point.

Stressors in the workplace

	Type	Potential stressors
	Physical environment	Lighting noise, smell, nearness to others, lack of access to natural light, temperature
Environment	Systems	Hierarchies, management style, appraisal, working hours, informal relationships
	Industrial relations	Turnover, disputes, accidents
	Perception	Experience, sex, culture, ethnic relations, social background, fear of success, fear of failure, mental health, status
Individual attitude	Relationships	Peers, superiors, subordinates, family ties
	Physical	Fitness, personal health, clothing
	Skill	Lack of training, communication skills, job design, job content
Work	Technology	Obsolete equipment, new equipment, wrong equipment

The cost of stress

Measuring the cost of stress is not easy. Stress results in a wide variety of physical and mental disorders, so that organizations trying to estimate the costs have a problem in assessing them. The best figures available indicate that 37 million working days each year are lost because of stress-related illness, at a cost to the British economy of £3,000 million – or 20 per cent of the GNP. Organizations which take the problem of stress seriously have identified all of these factors below as having their root cause in organizational dysfunctions, that is, the failure of the individual, the environment and the job to 'mesh'.

- absenteeism
- poor industrial relations
- poor productivity
- high staff turnover
- conflict and non-co-operation
- job dissatisfaction
- frequent accidents

Health and Safety at Work measures

In practice the UK Health and Safety at Work Act 1974 has been used by employers and trade unions alike as an opportunity to improve safety standards rather than health care. But the Act does include specific mention of mental health and the definition of personal injury as 'any disease and any impairment of a person's physical or mental condition.' It seems likely though that there may soon be a shift of emphasis, particularly as news of initiatives from the United States and from the Scandinavian countries becomes more widespread. In the US, for example, there are 'wear and tear' claims for work-related distress. In Sweden, the Working Environment Act 1977 stresses the importance of personal control over the working situation. Some of the main provisions of Norwegian legislation are given as an example.

Counting the costs

Companies which have introduced stress diagnosis and control programmes measure the results against significant factors – absenteeism, for example. Whatever the criteria, it appears that positive measures *do* have an effect on productivity and morale. Those who want to read more on the subject of cost and cost benefit will find *Coping with stress at work,* edited by Judi Marshall and Cary L. Cooper, particularly useful.

Counting the cost of work-related distress is not easy but indicates that distress is a significant cost to most organizations

The Norwegian Working Environment Act

General requirements

Technology, work organization, work times (for example, shift plans) and payment systems are to be designed so that negative physiological or psychological effects for employees are avoided as well as negative influences on the alertness necessary to the observance of safety considerations. Employees are to be given possibilities for personal development and for the maintenance and development of skills.

Design of jobs

In the planning of work and design of jobs, possibilities for employee self-determination and maintenance of skills are to be considered. Monotonous repetitive work, and work that is bound by machine or assembly line in such a way that there is no room left for variation in work rhythm, should be avoided. Jobs should be designed so as to give possibilities for variation, for contact with others, for understanding of the inter-dependence between elements that constitute a job, and for information and feedback to employees concerning production requirements and results.

Systems for planning and control (for example automatic data processing systems)

Workers or their elected representatives are to be kept informed about systems used for planning and control and any changes in such systems. They are to be given the training necessary to understand such systems and influence their design.

Mode of remuneration and risk to safety

Piece-rate payment and related forms of payment are not to be used if salaried systems can increase the safety level.

For all of us

- How can I measure the costs of stress in my organization?
- What can I do to mitigate the costs?

Selected reading

KOWALSKI, A. 'Stress in the workplace can cost you big money' in *Canadian Personnel and Industrial Relations Journal.* Vol. 26, No. 2, March 1979. pp 18–22.

People and work change

If there was one word to describe the 20th century and work attitudes then that word would be CHANGE. A recent study in *Fortune* magazine showed that major corporations are likely to undergo signficant restructuring every two or three years. If you add to that all the minor changes that typically take place – new staff, different equipment, altered procedures it quickly becomes evident that work change happens continually.

Resistance to change

Not all change is unwelcome – a holiday is unlikely to meet with resistance for example. But when the change is perceived to prevent or decrease a need satisfaction then conflict will arise. Such a change is seen as a threat to existing – and comfortable – habits. Even if the change has a positive advantage it may still provoke hostility because it alters the steady state or homeostasis. So, when the 'Office Bore' finally retires their absence may provoke a stress reaction simply because the equilibrium of the office has been disturbed!

Types of resistance

Resistance to change varies from person to person, in the same way that people respond to demands differently. Change is another demand placed upon us. Our response varies according to the number of other demands already placed upon us and our perceived ability to cope. The types of response range from a temporary disequilibrium to outright rebellion:

| Temporary disequilibrium followed by a quick adjustment | Apathy | Antagonism | Open opposition rebellion and destruction |

Change places additional demands upon people

Ask yourself

Line Manager

- Do I give my staff sufficient warning of planned change at work?
- Do I give my staff sufficient support in the event of unexpected change?

Trainer

- Do I work closely with Line Managers and Welfare Officers to minimize the undesirable aspects of change?
- Am I resistant to change in my working methods or environment?

Welfare Officer

- Do I work closely with Line Managers and Trainers to minimize the undesirable aspects of change?
- What can I do to lessen the potential stress of organizational change?

For all of us

- Am I unnecessarily resistant to change?
- What changes have I experienced recently which have caused me to feel stressed?

Your notes/personal points

Selected reading

STEWART, V. *Change: Challenge for management.* pp 83–85.

Change as a stressor

Change as we have seen increases the demands made upon people. Increasing demands has a direct effect upon performance. To understand this we need to appreciate that stressors have both a motivating and demotivating effect. There is a link between the number of stressors and the quality of performance. Have a look at the following diagram which illustrates this link:

- On the left-hand side of the model too few stressors have a negative effect upon performance

- The top curve represents the optimum where the amount of demand produces the best performance

- The right-hand side of the model shows the decline in performance as the number of stressors becomes too high for the person to cope with

  It is important to remember that individual tolerance to stressors varies so that one person's optimum will be another's breakdown.

Stressors and performance

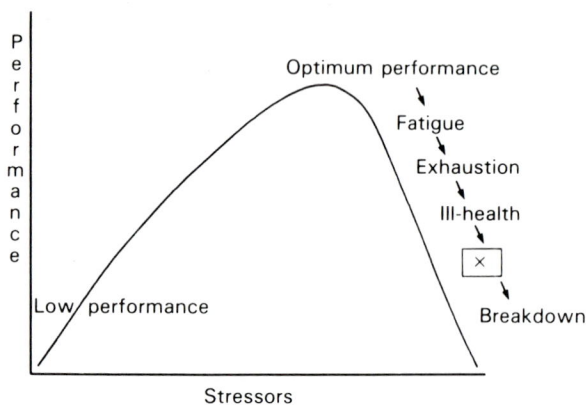

X is the point at which extra stressors may lead to breakdown.

Introducing change

Change is an additional stressors. Introduced at a time of low demands and low performance it can have a positive effect. At the wrong time though the result is more likely to be harmful unless it is introduced very carefully to minimize damage. You can find out more about introducing change in Section 4. Managing stress.

Introducing change can have both a positive and a negative effect upon performance

For all of us

- Do I always view change as potentially bad?
- What steps can I take to minimize the undesirable effects of change?

Your notes/personal points

Selected reading

HOWARD, R. W. *Coping and adapting*. pp 36–39.

The effect of technological change

In the last decade, with the introduction of the microprocessor, we have seen more changes in work technology (and particularly office technology) than in the previous fifty years. There are few aspects of work – desk-top publishing, electronic mail, teleconferencing, word-processing – that have been left untouched. Along with the undoubted benefits there has been a less welcome side effect: increased stress.

Technology as a stressor

As with any change new technology implies uncertainty and fear. It is hardly surprising therefore that the advent of the microprocessor has brought with it a host of stressors:

- difficulty in adapting, leading to tiredness and resentment
- increasing job complexity, often with no increase in pay
- a downgrading of work conditions – less mobility and a decrease in social contact at work, due to being tied to the screen
- fears of ill-health – eyestrain, effects of radiation, backache, etc
- fears of job obsolescence
- role ambiguities as traditional barriers blur
- decreasing career prospects if the technology is unfamiliar or not understood
- fears of job downgrading – the machine does it all

Actual or imagined, these stressors are very real for many people when faced with the introduction of technological change. Simply emphasising the positive benefits of a new piece of equipment will do little to counteract fears. Managers must be aware of the likelihood of stress and take steps to meet and allay fears honestly, through consultation, discussion and training. Identifying the impact of a change *before* it occurs is crucial if the stressor effect is to be mitigated.

Technological change introduces efficiency benefits but may also bring about distress unless the change is carefully handled

Ask yourself

Line Manager

- Do I regard technological change as a potential threat to my work, role, or status?
- Am I fully aware of the extent of technological change affecting my own department?
- How does this compare with other departments?

Trainer

- How can training be used to offset the potentially harmful effects of technological change?
- Am I personally happy with the technological changes affecting the training world?

Welfare Officer

- Am I prepared to counsel personal fears about technological change?

For all of us

- Do I create problems for myself by believing that I cannot cope with technological change?
- What positive steps can I take?

Your notes/personal points

Selected reading

COX, S. *Change and stress in the modern office.* Further Education Unit Occasional Paper. pp 22–23.

Changes in the workforce

Over the last 30 years there have been significant changes in the structure of the workforce: 24 per cent work part-time, unemployment has trebled; women constitute 44 per cent of the workforce; 68 per cent of women work and full-time jobs have decreased. At the same time new patterns of working – shift work, flexible hours and a move from traditional manufacturing industry to the service sector have emerged. In the public sector there has also been a shift in values to an emphasis on cost-effectiveness and the introduction of the profit motive. These fundamental changes have implications for all of us, in that they create uncertainty, confusion and ambiguity, about roles and about goals.

Goal ambiguity

This occurs when there is uncertainty about what it is we are trying to achieve or when the goal becomes meaningless. People know that the systems and methods which have served well in the past can no longer continue to do so but also know that changing to meet the future is liable to be difficult and threatening – especially if that change involves 'slimming down' the workforce. The Bell Telephone Company in the States provides a classic example of goal ambiguity when they achieved in the 1970s their goal of 'a telephone in every home'. It took many years before the company was able to redefine its goals – during which time morale reached rock-bottom. Personal goals also became outdated and confused.

Role ambiguity

As reorganizations come and go people become increasingly confused about their jobs and position in the hierarchy. Change which involves reporting relationships also creates ambiguity, either when a superior/subordinate relationship is altered or when a person is asked to report to more than one person.

Implications

Ignoring the stressor effect of changes in work and patterns of work gives rise to unnecessary and avoidable conflict. Change must be introduced carefully taking all the implications into account – not just those which are the direct result of it.

Changes in the work force and work patterns create ambiguity

Ask yourself

Line manager

- Am I clear about the main purpose of my own work and that of the people who work for me?
- Do I make sure that everyone who works for me is clear about their main purpose?

Trainer

- Is my own goal and role within the organization clear?
- How can I help other people define and understand their goals and roles?

Welfare Officer

- Can I take a strategic role to help define goals and roles?

For all of us

- Am I clear about my work role and goals?
- If not, where can I get help in defining them?

Your notes/personal points

Women at work

Women face peculiar stressors at work, particularly when they are in certain occupations, for example engineering, or when they are in management positions, which are not viewed as 'women's work'. Women form some 44 per cent of the work force – yet, despite the Sex Discrimination and Equal Pay Acts, still suffer from the arbitrary division between 'men's work' and 'women's work', earning only 74 per cent of men's hourly rate.

Role conflict and work expectations

Most people are familiar with the implicit and explicit sexism that faces many women at work. The usual response to a charge of sexism is to shrug it off with a laugh or an embarrassed shuffling of the feet. Such a response fails to recognise the stressor effect of the conflict that many women face between their expectations and the reality of their lives. Such stressors include:

- home/work conflict
- low expectations
- fear of success
- tokenism
- mobility problems
- childcare
- male-dominated organization
- stereotyping
- 'superwoman' syndrome
- high expectations
- lack of assertion
- sexual harrassment
- discrimination
- fewer training opportunities
- low pay/low status
- promotion blocks

Redressing the balance

This brief list of stressors serves to emphasise that the socialization of women is very different from that of men. Women are still seen in their role of carer, men in the role of breadwinner. Trying to compete under these additional handicaps imposed by society adds extra stressors for working women in addition to the 'normal' organizational stressors.

Women at work suffer additional stressors

Ask yourself

Line Manager

- Do I recognise that sexist attitudes can make life difficult for my female staff?
- Do I take active steps to combat this?

Trainer

- Do I take positive steps to confront and discuss sexist attitudes?
- Am I aware of the latest developments in women's training?

Welfare Officer

- What proportions of women are employed at various grades in my department?
- What is the balance between female clients and male clients with work related problems?

Your notes/personal points

Selected reading
COOPER, C. L. and DAVIDSON, M. J. *High pressure: Working lives of women managers.* Chapter 1.

Overload and underload

The amount of work content is an important stressor. Too much and we reach the top of the performance curve and have nowhere to go but down. Too little and we become equally stressed because our expectations are not being met. Obviously we can all cope with short periods of both over- and underload – it is when the period is extended that we are heading for trouble.

Underload and overload can be both 'quantitative' – when there is too much or too little to do – and 'qualitative' – when our abilities are not being used to the full or when the performance standards are too high.

Implications

There is an old adage which says 'you can't fit a square peg into a round hole'. So it is with people and their work. Individuals have different responses to different demands. Putting a person who wants a challenging job into one where they are unable to express their abilities is as dangerous as asking an unqualified person to cope with the demands of a medical practice. On the one hand there is underload, on the other overload. The bored housewife will be just as stressed as the over-worked executive. Those who are responsible for the recruitment, welfare and development of staff must consider if the work that people are asked to perform is liable to produce underload or overload for each individual that they are responsible for.

Effects on performance

Work which is wrongly weighted for the individual can result in performance deficiency, poor decision-making, increased accidents, absenteeism and increased alcohol and cigarette consumption. Have another look at the performance curve on page 56 to remind yourself of the link between stressors and performance.

Overload and underload over a sustained period will result in performance deterioration

Ask yourself

Line Manager

- Do I make sure that I choose the right person for the job?
- Do I help the people that work for me to find the right working balance?

Trainer

- Can I help managers understand the crucial importance of the best possible match between the individual and the job?

Welfare Officer

- Do I recommend transfer when the individual is unfitted for their work?
- Do accident or other problem statistics indicate a mismatch between people and jobs?

For all of us

- What can I do to reduce the pressure?

Your notes/personal points

Selected reading

IVANCEVICH, J. M. and MATTESON, M. T. *Stress and work: A managerial perspective.* pp 112–114.

Shiftwork and unsocial hours

The effects of shiftwork and unsocial hours are potentially extremely stressful. Shiftwork disrupts 'normal' life in both a biological and a social sense. Those who have to work nights are not catered for: shops are closed, television shuts down – all the hundred and one facets of life that day workers take for granted are not available to night workers. Together with the disruption to family and social life the shiftworker is in a constant state of adaptation: adaptation to new sleep patterns, to new digestive rhythms. Even those who work permanent nights rarely adapt fully, because on their rest days they revert to normal behaviour patterns – hence when they return to work they have to readapt.

There is an assumption that the longer someone works shifts the easier it becomes. In fact there is evidence that the opposite is the case. Long-term shiftworking becomes harder to cope with as the body rebels against the constant demand for adaptation. Those who are younger generally find it easier to adjust to the demands of shiftworking – many experts recommend that people in their forties and fifties should not take up shiftwork because of the problems of adaptation.

Symptoms associated with shiftwork stress

Not all shiftworkers suffer from stress. Some are able to adapt or find that the benefits – more time at home when their children are awake for example – compensate for the frustrations. There are however certain symptoms of shiftwork stress that are more pronounced in those who work standard hours:

- chronic fatigue
- lassitude
- aggression
- irritability
- insomnia
- depression

In addition it seems that while the rate of accidents at work is roughly similar between day and night workers, accidents at night are more severe.

So debilitating are the possible effects of shiftwork that it is banned in some countries – Belgium, Norway and Sweden for example – except where a joint trade union/employer agreement has been reached that the nightwork is essential.

Shiftworking imposes special stressors upon employees

Ask yourself

Line Manager and Trainer

- Do I need to take the effects of shiftwork or unsocial hours into consideration?

Welfare Officer

- Are there any shiftworkers in my department?
- Do accident rates differ between this group and other groups?

Your notes/personal points

Selected reading

MCDONALD, N. and DOYLE, M. *The stresses of work*. Chapter 4.

Approaching retirement

Paradoxically, retirement can be both a major stressor and a way of coping with work-related stress. The transition to retirement and its effect depends on the perception of the individual concerned. If the impending retirement is seen as offering positive advantages – increased leisure – then the stressor effect of finishing work will be much less than for the person for whom work has been a major focus. There is a myth that when we reach retirement most of us suffer an instant health decline because we are no longer 'useful'. In fact, the evidence is that retirement cannot be associated directly with health decline for the majority of 'retirees'. When problems do occur they can usually be related to specific aspects of the retiree's life rather than retirement itself – bereavement for example. But the most usual finding is that three quarters of retirees enjoy their retirement, once the initial adaptation stage is completed.

Retirement stressors

Nevertheless there are stressors associated with finishing work. Appreciating that they exist is important both for those who are about to retire and for their managers. Many organizations now operate pre-retirement courses as a way of mitigating the more stressful aspects of retirement. Such stressors include:

- fear of the unknown
- loss of self-esteem
- diminished status
- loss of purpose
- fear of ill-health
- reduced income
- loneliness
- non-achievement of career hopes

These must be weighed against the positive aspects of retirement:

- increased leisure
- more contact with family
- removal of work stressors
- opportunities for self-development

A major life event

Retirement is a major life event, implying enormous upheaval. The more we measure our status and esteem by our work, the more difficult it will be for us to cope with the demands of retirement. It depends on our personal values – how we balance the positive and negative aspects – as to the effect retirement will have upon us.

Retirement can both increase and decrease stress

Ask yourself

Line Manager

- Do I help members of my staff to prepare themselves for retirement?

Trainer

- Can training help to reduce the stress effect of retirement?

Welfare Officer

- Do I liaise effectively with trainers and line managers in preparing people for retirement?

Your notes/personal points

Selected reading

BEEHR, T. A. and BHAGAT, R. S. (ed.) *Human stress and cognition in organizations: An integrated perspective.* Chapter 7.

Management style and communication

Surveys of organizational stressors have concluded that the management style has a major part to play in reducing or increasing stress. Research indicates that organizations which adopt an involving and participative management style are more successful in maintaining motivation and morale. Involvement is the key to reducing uncertainty and fear about ambiguity and change.

Participation

Participation of itself may well be a stressor when introduced into an organization which has long existed using an autocratic style. Managers may be unsure of the skills required for participative management and may feel that their authority is threatened. Staff may react with suspicion if they are involved when no involvement took place before.

Nonetheless, increasing involvement eventually relieves some of the distress of people in organizations by opening up new avenues for self-expression and creativity. Non-involvement increases anxiety and tension. It introduces a 'competition of knowledge' – 'I know what is going on and you don't' – which diverts staff from their work.

Characteristics of management style

AUTOCRATIC/ LOW PARTICIPATION	Encourages interpersonal competition, rigid hierarchy, impersonal communication, lack of communication, decisions made with little or no consultation, focus on individual achievements, reliance on procedure and rules, few opportunities for creativity.
DEMOCRATIC/ HIGH INVOLVEMENT	Encourages personal expression, stresses teamwork, values creativity, encourages self-development, makes joint decisions, is flexible, places high value on formal and informal communications.

Management style plays a key factor in reducing or increasing stress

Ask yourself

Line Manager

- Is my management style one which reduces or increases stress for people at work?
- Do I involve my staff enough in what is going on?

Trainer

- Do management courses contain information on the advantages of a participative style of management?

Welfare Officer

- Is there any perceptible link between specific sections/managers and problems with which I have to deal?

For all of us

- If my manager's style causes me a problem should I discuss it with them?
- Am I sufficiently aware of the potential effect of my behaviour on other people?

Your notes/personal points

Selected reading

COOPER, C. L. and PAYNE, R. (ed.) *Stress at work.* pp 92–93.

Is stress inevitable?

From this brief overview of social, personal and work stressors it might appear that stress is unavoidable. Of course this is not the case. All sorts of factors determine not only if we are *likely* to become stressed, but also *what* will cause us to feel stressed. The workaholic for example is likely to find underemployment more stressful than being overloaded with work. Our response to stressors is very much an individual reaction, determined by our background, our culture and our heredity.

The factors that we have examined may cause distress to *some* but not *all* individuals. Nevertheless it is important to take their stress potential seriously and to look for ways to lessen likely stressors. That way we will all get the most out of our lives.

Recognising your personal stress level is something that cannot be done for you – there is no magic formula that says X+Y = stress. The Life Events Inventory and the Job Stress Questionnaire can only point directions to assist you in deciding what is – and what is not – potentially stressful in your own life.

Job stress questionnaire

Circle the number that best reflects the degree to which the particular statement applies to you. 'O' equals an unstressed state and '6' equals a highly stressed state.

For all of us

- Do I ever feel stressed by my work?
- Do I recognise which factors are the stressful ones?
- Can I take any steps to improve matters?
- Can I get help from other people?

Your notes/personal points

Stress factors	Stress						
	Low						High
Relationship with boss	0	1	2	3	4	5	6
Relationships with colleagues	0	1	2	3	4	5	6
Work overload	0	1	2	3	4	5	6
Work underload	0	1	2	3	4	5	6
Making mistakes	0	1	2	3	4	5	6
Feeling undervalued	0	1	2	3	4	5	6
Time pressures	0	1	2	3	4	5	6
Promotion prospects	0	1	2	3	4	5	6
Being relocated	0	1	2	3	4	5	6
Taking work home	0	1	2	3	4	5	6
Pay	0	1	2	3	4	5	6
Policy administration	0	1	2	3	4	5	6
Lack of power and influence	0	1	2	3	4	5	6
Lack of consultation and communication	0	1	2	3	4	5	6
Job ambiguity	0	1	2	3	4	5	6
Top management being remote	0	1	2	3	4	5	6

Section 4.
Managing stress

Contents

Using this section

This section can be used in two ways:

- If you are new to the subject of stress you will find it helpful to read through the whole section

- On the other hand you will find it useful to dip into this section as a reminder. For example, you may want to use one of the questionnaires for yourself or with colleagues

To help you dip into, or skim read, the material, each topic has a clear heading and the **Key point** is picked out in bold type.

By the time you have completed this section you will be able to:

- identify methods of coping with stress

- examine methods of managing your own stress

- understand the value of self-help in controlling stress

- be familiar with techniques useful for alleviating organizational stress

Where appropriate, reading relevant to the subject matter is listed for your information.

Introduction

Accepting our stress

Everyone responds differently to stressors. A change in the office layout may be a blessing to one person and totally unacceptable to another. So there is no way that we can eliminate all the stressors in our environments, but we can learn methods of coping with them. Because we are all different, each of us has to find our own preferred methods of dealing with distress – so don't worry if certain relaxation techniques don't work for you. Try some of the many others available.

How we can help

There are a number of approaches to coping with stress, which we can gather under the general title of 'stress-proofing'. Stress-proofing simply means managing ourselves better, so that we are not so overwhelmed by demands that our eustress (the level of stress we all need to survive) becomes distress. Methods of stress-proofing include:

- reducing and avoiding
- training to meet stressors
- developing resilience

In this section we shall be looking at all three approaches. Some or all of the techniques discussed may be useful. A prerequisite for success, though, depends on recognition of stress, or likely stress, which means taking seriously the debilitating effects of stress, refusing to accept them as an inevitable and unchanging part of our lives. Stress is not pre-ordained; neither should it be ignored as a 'fashionable' topic. Without intervention stress can kill.

Different people will find different ways to cope with stress

Think positive

Much of our reaction to the stressors in our environment depends on our own feelings of being able to cope. If we adopt a negative attitude we are much more likely to suffer than if we retain a sense of faith in our own coping ability. Taking positive action simply means believing that we *do* have a control over our own destiny and that we *can* fight back. That's why we emphasise the value of positive thought as a starting point for coping.

Faulty thinking

If positive thought is so important it follows that negative or faulty thinking has to be recognised before we can begin to think positively. Faulty thinking includes:

- seeing things in black and white, as either 'good' or 'bad'

- overgeneralising – 'Mary doesn't like me therefore I am unlikeable'

- always expecting the worst

- always expecting the best

- believing we are the centre of events – 'It's all my fault'

- believing I'm always wrong and that I don't count

Correcting faulty thinking

Below, techniques for counteracting faulty thinking are identified, together with their anticipated result. What they have in common is that they demand objective rather than subjective analysis. Regaining objectivity is the key to positive thought.

For all of us

- Does my less-than-positive attitude contribute to my stress?

- How can I develop a more positive attitude?

___

Your notes/personal points

___

Selected reading

HOWARD, R. W. *Coping and adapting: How you can learn to cope with stress.* Chapter 10.

Coping with faulty thinking

Technique	Method	Result
Look ahead	Work out the very best/very worst that can happen in a situation.	We regain a perspective. There is no longer a fear of the unknown.
Reapportion liability/ blame	Work out who/what else is involved that will have an impact on results.	Realise that because there are other factors the outcome of a situation won't be 'all our fault'.
Refocus	Ask, listen, involve, discover that other people have the same sorts of fears and worries.	Realise that we haven't been 'singled out' by fate – other people have similar doubts or fears.
Step back	Analyse a situation factually to clarify assumptions.	Reveals that our judgements are often based on 'feelings' rather than truth.
Test	Try out a belief, eg 'I can't use a computer, I'm not mathematically minded.'	Reveals that 'logical' beliefs about oneself are irrational when practically tested.

Regaining objectivity is the key to positive thought and action

Positive action

Once we have recognised that we are suffering from stress we must take some action. Obvious as this sounds it is often the sticking point for many of us. While we know that there is a problem, we often find it hard to find a solution that we can live with. Positive thinking is one answer, as is defining the problem and setting goals. Part of the reason for holding back from taking action is simply that there are so many people offering solutions that we become overwhelmed with choices and end up by doing nothing – or attempting to do too much.

Defining the problem

Analysing the stressor and defining possible solutions can relieve the situation. For example, if we take a common stressor 'work overload', we can list the reasons for the overload which may include:

- lack of staff
- poor time management
- taking on too much
- not delegating enough
- not having the right skills
- not being able to say no

Defining the problem means that we are half way to finding a solution. So, if we decide that the root cause of our difficulty is that we are taking on too much, we can list possible coping strategies:

- delegate more
- learn to say no

Both strategies present a solution that we can work towards. We might decide that we need some assertiveness training to help us refuse the extra work that is being thrust upon us.

Problem solving

Problem solving is something that most of us are not very skilled at. We tend to see our problems as insoluble, or we look for very traditional solutions, or we blame other people. It can often be helpful to 'brainstorm' solutions with others, to look for answers that may help. Brainstorming is simply listing solutions as we think of them, without comment or evaluation, so that thoughts flow freely. Only when all the possibilities have been exhausted do we then examine the ideas.

Evaluating solutions

Of course, once we have produced our list of possible solutions we then have to evaluate them. This is a personal process, but it is important not to dismiss possible solutions because of faulty thinking – the 'I couldn't possibly do that' syndrome. So we need to apply some ratings to our solutions and test them for acceptability. One very easy way of doing this is to take each answer and list the 'plus' and 'minus' points. If we return to our original example:

Solution	Plus	Minus
Delegate more	Gives staff more responsibility; trains staff; lets me get on with major tasks; could improve staff relationships.	May have to spend more time on training; may increase mistakes; may lose authority.

Since there are more 'plus' than 'minus' points, it seems, in this case, that the solution of delegating should be the one we implement. Of course there may be major drawbacks to a solution which might outweigh the fact that there are more 'pluses' than 'minuses', and vice versa. If a possible solution really is unworkable then you simply move through your list until you find one that you can live with.

Ask yourself

- Is there a particular problem which is affecting me now that could benefit from analysis?
- Why do I avoid taking positive action?

Your notes/personal points

Selected reading

RICKARDS, T. *Problem solving through creative analysis*. Chapter 5.

Avoiding situations

One aspect of taking positive action that we haven't yet explored is that of avoidance. Not all situations can be avoided, in which case we need to analyse them for possible solutions. But some can – but many of us adopt an almost masochistic streak by deliberately putting ourselves into situations which we *know* will cause us stress. Such action is plain foolishness – even small children learn very quickly that putting their hands in the fire will only cause them unnecessary pain!

Analysing the situation

Avoiding stressful situations means we have to know what causes us to feel most stressed. Completing the questionnaires in this booklet will provide a starting point. In addition it is helpful to spend a little time thinking about the situations, things, and events which personally stress us. Anything which causes us to feel anxious, angry, frightened or frustrated is a potential stressor and should be included.

Making the change

Once we have listed the potential stressors in our lives, we can examine them dispassionately to see if there are any which we can actively avoid. For example, if catching a crowded train to and from work is a problem, we might be able to avoid the situation by catching an earlier or later one – or change our method of transport – perhaps to cycling or car-sharing. All of us have the power to do a great deal to reorganize our lives to minimise stress – all it takes is a little forethought.

Analyse potentially stressful situations for ways of avoiding them

Use the grid below to:
- list situations you find stressful
- define exactly what they make you feel
- suggest avoiding action

Your notes/personal points

Selected reading

BOOTH, A. L. *Stressmanship.* pp 184–191.

Stressor	Effect it has on me	Possible avoiding action
At home?		
At work?		
In social situations?		

Taking control – assertion

There are many situations in our everyday lives where we either lose control and become angry or, alternatively, say nothing and keep our true feelings hidden. Both types of behaviour are potential stressors, particularly if they become our usual way of reacting to difficult situations. Surprisingly, although aggressive and submissive behaviours appear to be at opposite ends of the spectrum, both often stem from the same root cause of feelings or personal inadequacy. Both are a response mechanism to counteract a perceived threat. In the short term each produces the feeling that we have coped with 'danger'. In the longer term the effect is to reinforce our low self-esteem as we lose the respect of others by our extreme behaviour.

What is assertion?

Assertion is a much misunderstood word. It is *not* about getting our own way all the time. It *is* about being honest in our relationships, self-confident and rational. In a nutshell it is about having respect for ourselves and for others. It includes recognition of basic human rights, particularly the right to say 'no' and the right to make mistakes. Being self-confident is the basis of assertion.

Is assertion easy?

Learning to be assertive is not easy. We are all products of our backgrounds and have as a result made (often mistaken) judgements about ourselves and our abilities. How often, for example, have you heard yourself say 'yes' to a request which you didn't want to undertake, but were afraid to say 'no' to? Or reacted by finding a million and one excuses rather than being straightforward in your refusal. Nevertheless it is worth the effort. On the following page you will see a basic list of rights. Putting them into practice will improve inter-personal relationships for all of us.

Assertive behaviour recognises that having respect for ourselves and for others is a basic human right

Consider your rights

1. I choose to have the right to state my own needs and set my own priorities as a person, independent of any roles that I may assume in life.

2. I choose to have the right to be treated with respect as an intelligent and equal human being.

3. I choose to have the right to express my feelings.

4. I choose to have the right to express my opinions and values.

5. I choose to have the right to say 'no' or 'yes' for myself.

6. I choose to have the right to make mistakes and be responsible for them.

7. I choose to have the right to change my mind.

8. I choose to have the right to say 'I don't understand' and to ask for more information.

9. I choose to have the right to ask for what I want.

10. I choose to have the right to decline the responsibility for other people's problems.

11. I choose to have the right to deal with others without being dependent on them for approval.

12. I choose to have the right not to assert myself.

13. I choose to have the right to refuse requests without feeling guilty or selfish.

14. I choose to have the right to be successful.

15. I choose to have the right to be left alone.

Reprinted with permission from Glenna Sutcliffe of Structured Learning Courses, 17 Athol Road, Bramhall, Stockport.

Which of these basic rights do I regularly deny myself?

Selected reading

PAUL, N. 'Assertiveness without tears: A training programme for executive equality' in *Personnel Management*. April 1979. pp 37–40.

Relaxation and breathing

Many of us tend to dismiss relaxation and breathing as a technique for controlling stress because we believe that they are time-consuming and smack slightly of esoteric religious beliefs. In fact there are many different ways we can learn to relax. Some can take many years to master fully but others are very straightforward and, with a little practice, can soon become part of our daily lives.

Why relaxation and breathing are important

When we respond to stressors our muscles tense and our breathing quickens as we prepare for 'flight or fight'. Such a response is perfectly proper when faced with a real physical danger – a poisonous snake for example. Unfortunately we have the same response to any stressor – waiting for an interview or speaking in public. Our bodies prepare for an action which isn't forthcoming. Breathing is the only automatic bodily function over which we can exercise some control and by doing so we can decrease our inappropriate stress responses, and return to equilibrium.

Learning control

Most of the literature on stress and stress management includes examples of breathing and relaxation exercises. Some are very complex, others extremely simple. We describe two simple exercises which will help you to control your stress responses. It is important that you practice the exercises so that you can call upon them when needed. We suggest 5–15 minutes a day as about right. Try to practice somewhere warm and quiet. Wear loose clothing in which you feel comfortable. Don't try and force results – it can be helpful to 'step outside' yourself and observe how you are reacting. There are a number of 'relaxation tapes' available and these too may be useful for you.

Relaxation and breath control play a major part in dampening down inappropriate stress responses

Relaxation exercises

These are only a 'taster' and are intended to show how simple such exercises can be. Any good book on stress management and control will provide plenty of other exercises you can use. Exercises like these can be practised both individually or as part of a class – perhaps during lunch-hours.

Calming breathing

- Sit back comfortably in a chair, with your shoulders relaxed. Imagine there is a string on top of your head pulling you up gently. Take five deep steady breaths.
- Breathe in through your nose for a count of four; feeling your abdomen rise.
- Pause.
- Breathe out through your nose for a count of four; feeling your abdomen fall.
- Continue until you feel yourself calming down.
- This is a useful technique for steadying yourself – during a traffic jam or before an interview for example.

Floppy doll

- You can do this either sitting on an armless chair or standing up.
- Take ten deep slow breaths from the abdomen.
- Each time you breathe out begin to flop forward at the head and neck.
- Continue breathing slowly letting your shoulders and arms fall forward until you are dangling like a floppy doll.
- Rest in that position for a minute or two.
- Come up very slowly, breathing gently from the abdomen.
- Rest for as long as you can manage, still breathing slowly and deeply.
- Take a deep breath and you will feel refreshed and alert.
- This is a useful exercise for switching off the stress response. Use it after a heavy day so that you can get the most from your leisure time.

Selected reading

MADDERS, J. *Stress and relaxation.*

72

Discharging skills

One of the most marked cultural traits of British society is the difficulty we all have in showing emotions. It seems that maintaining a 'stiff upper lip' in the face of adversity is a prized skill, and that it is not quite cricket to express our true feelings! Which is all very laudible except that such behaviour of itself produces extra demands for us to cope with. After all, there is more than enough potential for stress in losing a job without our adding to it by pretending that it doesn't really matter that much! If we are honest, most of us can think of many times when we have curbed our real feelings in order to 'protect' ourselves.

What are discharging skills?

Discharging skills are simply being able to produce an appropriate response to situations. So when we are sad we cry; when we are happy we laugh. Sounds simple – but when did you last have a really good belly laugh? Or cry when you were seriously upset? Yet there is increasing evidence that both tears and laughter have a real therapeutic effect. For example, it appears that tears can speed up the healing process for injuries. And some cancer therapists insist that a positive attitude can halt the spread of cancerous cells.

What about anger?

Uncontrolled anger can have a seriously debilitating effect on the digestive system. Conversely, the same is true of anger which is kept under tight control. Both are inappropriate responses. A useful technique is to discharge anger as quickly as possible – throw something at a wall, work it out through vigorous exercise – and then replace the anger with positive emotions. Use the Calming Breathing exercise or count to ten. Remember though to discharge the anger against an *inanimate* object – this is not the time to involve others! Finally, once you have calmed down try to analyse what happened to make you angry. Ask yourself if the anger was justified; or, if you over-reacted, promise yourself that next time things will be different.

Expressing our emotions is a useful method of mitigating stress

Ask yourself

Line Manager

- Do I expect my staff to hide behind a 'stiff upper lip' all the time?
- Do I feel that showing emotion is only for junior members of staff?
- Do I feel that showing emotion is a sign of weakness?

Trainer

- Do I encourage my trainees to express their emotions?
- Am I prepared to express my own emotions in a group when appropriate?

Welfare Officer

- Do I feel that my emotions are of lesser importance than those of my clients?

For all of us

- Should I be using my emotions more positively?

Your notes/personal points

Selected quote

To cure the mind's wrong bias, Spleen,
Some recommend the bowling green;
Some, hilly walks; all, exercise;
Fling but a stone, the giant dies;
Laugh and be well.

Matthew Green, 1696–1737

The value of exercise

Increasing our level of physical fitness will do a great deal to overcome stress. Exercise will:

- fulfil the action demanded by the 'fight or flight' response and so reduce the numbers of unwanted fats and sugars in our bodies

- make our bodies stronger and better able to cope with the debilitating effects of stress

- increase our energy and our stamina

Nowadays most of us are more than aware that exercise and physical fitness are important. To an extent we may be suffering from 'exercise overkill' – we read and hear so much that we respond negatively. Unfortunately, much as we might want to pretend otherwise, exercise does have a positive value. Assess your level of fitness using the easy questionnaire opposite. If it reveals that you could be fitter, then consider taking up some form of exercise which you enjoy. Remember that exercise doesn't have to be confined to sporting activities. You can get a great deal of benefit from simple changes to your life style – cycling to work instead of taking the train for example. Finally, if you think you are seriously unfit you should always seek the advice of your GP before embarking upon an exercise programme.

If you still have some doubts about the value of exercise a quick look at the following statistics might help to convince you:

During the years 1968–70, 17,944 middle-aged men in six government departments across Britain participated in a study of the incidence of coronary heart-disease. Conclusions of this study indicate that:

- vigorous exercise in leisure-time is a protection against coronary heart disease.

- fatal heart attacks are less than half as common in 'vigorous exercise sportsmen' aged 40–65.

- at every age grouping for both fatal and non-fatal first heart attacks, those who practised vigorous exercise or sporting activities had lower rates.

Reprinted from *Why Harry?,* issued by the Medical Advisory Service of the Northern Ireland Civil Service.

Mens sana in corpore sano (A healthy mind in a healthy body)

How fit are you?

Does your job involve a lot of movement?	YES	NO
Are you on your feet for 2–3 hours every day?	YES	NO
Do you always climb the stairs rather than using the lift	YES	NO
Do you cycle or walk regularly?	YES	NO
Do you take any other form of vigorous exercise?	YES	NO
Do you exercise at least once a week?	YES	NO
Do you lift something heavy every day?	YES	NO
Do you tackle something strenuous every day?	YES	NO

Scoring

Score one point for every 'yes' answer

6–8 High fitness

4–5 Moderate fitness

0–3 Low fitness

Ask yourself

- Should I be taking more exercise?
- What form of exercise would I enjoy?

Your notes/personal points

Selected reading

3D Plan: Food, fitness and feelings. Issued by the Blue Band Programme for Positive Health.

Choosing a sensible diet

Together with exercise, getting our diet right is an obvious 'must' for stressproofing. Nowadays we are bombarded with information about what we should and should not eat. Often we get conflicting advice – 'milk is good for you', 'milk is full of fat which is bad for you'. Trying to sort out fact from fiction is time consuming and difficult – everyday something seems to change. But taking a positive attitude to the food we eat can only improve our general health, giving us more energy and more confidence.

What is a balanced diet?

Very simply, a balanced diet is one that combines moderate amounts from each of these four groups:

- milk and cheese
- meat and eggs and pulses or other protein sources
- fruit and vegetables
- breads and cereals

Ensuring that we eat foods from each group daily will provide a healthy and a balanced diet.

What should I avoid?

No foods are bad for us – it is *excess* that gives us problems. A diet composed entirely of fruit juice will not provide the carbohydrates and fats that our bodies need to function – quite apart from the likelihood that the acidity of the juice will rot our teeth! So the key words are 'moderation' and 'variety'.

A positive attitude to our diet can only give us more energy and confidence to cope with the stresses in our lives

Ask yourself

Line Manager

- Do I ensure that my staff take the meal breaks to whch they are entitled?
- Do I have any members of staff who may not be eating correctly?

Trainer

- Do I ensure that trainees get time to eat properly while attending a training event?
- Do I eat properly when running one?

Welfare Officer

- Do I ensure that good advice about diet and nutrition is made available to all staff?

For all of us

- Do I take the time to plan and eat a balanced diet?
- In what way do I need to improve my eating habits?

Your notes/personal points

Selected reading

BOOTH, A. L. *Stressmanship.* Chapter 12.

Controlling time

For many people, time – or rather the lack of it – is an enormous stressor. It is no coincidence that the major characteristics of Type 'A' personalities is 'hurry sickness'—the feeling that there are never enough hours in the day to achieve all their goals. And as work pressures increase, they feel more and more strained. They seem to be controlled *by* time rather than able to control it.

Time management is taking control

Taking control of our time is easy. All we have to do is:

- find out how we use our time now

- use the lessons learnt to organize ourselves more productively.

Of course, it does require spending a little time – but the benefits far outweigh the slight inconvenience!

Organizing for time management

Using a time log is the key to finding out how we *really* use our time – not how we *think* we use it. Recording our actual time-use points out a number of areas where, with just a little forethought and planning, we can make better use of time. An example follows which can be copied and used. You will notice that there is a box for recording which activities were interruptions to a task. This is because most of us at work tend to welcome any interruption – the odd cup of coffee, someone popping in for a chat. Analysing our interruptions can be a salutary lesson for us all, providing we then take steps to structure our days to minimize them. Once the time log has been kept for a period – a week is the suggested minimum – it can be analysed by asking these questions of each task:

- did I need to do that task at all?

- if the answer is 'yes' – did I need to do it then?

- do I avoid major tasks in favour of less important ones?

Tips for time management

- delegate
- control interruptions
- use a daily action plan
- set objectives
- handle paper only once
- train staff better
- prioritize tasks
- learn to say 'no'
- learn to speed-read
- do it now

Time management is simply learning to organize ourselves

Keeping a time log

Example

Day	Monday		Interruption
Time	Task	Yes	No
9.00	Coffee		
9.15	Wrote letters to clients		
9.16	Mary with report		
9.18	Read reports		
9.30	Wrote letters		
9.35	Went to loo		

Day			Interruption
Time	Task	Yes	No

Ask yourself

What is my main time-thief?

Your notes/personal points

Finding the right work

An important stressor for many of us is job dissatisfaction. Of course, finding the right work isn't easy these days but we can all take steps to *improve* the content of our present jobs. Common reasons for dissatisfaction include:

- having too much to do
- having too little to do
- find the work too difficult
- finding the work too easy
- too much public contact
- not enough public contact
- poor working conditions

In each case the first steps to remedying the situation are in our own hands. We have to ask:

- can I do anything to change the situation?
- who can I talk to – Line Manager, Trainer, Welfare Officer, anyone else?
- what else can be done?

Simply deciding what can be done and then discussing it can often point the way to changing either the context or the content of our work to make us feel less unhappy. For example, it may be possible to transfer to a different section; take on more interesting work or undertake training. So it is crucial that we *communicate* our worries; *listen* to any solutions and *take action.*

Moving on

If there genuinely is no way out of the problem then we have to consider either looking for a new job or finding a leisure interest which will provide us with the satisfaction we are missing at work. Career counselling and training will both improve your chances of finding the right work.

We have to take the first steps to finding the right work ourselves

Ask yourself

Line Manager

- Are any of my staff square pegs in round holes?
- If so, what positive action should I take?

Trainer

- Do I have a responsibility to liaise with line management over obvious mismatches of person and work?
- As work demands change do I update my training to stay in line?

Welfare Officer

- Am I working sufficiently closely with line management to ensure that recruitment is effective?
- Do I use transfer as a positive option?

For all of us

- Am I in the right job?
- Would further training or development ensure a better match between me and my job?

___

Your notes/personal points

___

Selected reading

IVANCEVICH, J. M. and MATTESSON, M. T. *Stress and work: A managerial perspective.* pp 115–116.

Getting help from others

Once we have identified what is causing us to feel distressed, it may well be that we need to seek the help of others to resolve our problem. For many of us, this can provide a major barrier. We don't want to be seen as weak or inadequate, so, rather than admit to difficulty, we try to struggle on alone and usually fail. To put this into perspective, we can use the analogy of the car. Most of us are well able to carry out minor repairs – changing the wheel and the like – but when it comes to something more complex – replacing the clutch – we hand it over to the experts. If we can do this for our cars then it makes sense to do the same for our own bodies. Which is more important – saving face or getting better?

Who can help?

The list of possible sources of help is endless. The more obvious ones include:

- friends and relations
- the boss
- the Welfare Officer
- voluntary organizations such as:
  Marriage Guidance
  Alcoholics Anonymous
- the Samaritans
- your GP
- local radio 'Care Lines'

At the back of this book you will find a list of organizations who may be able to help.

What to do at work

At work, the first line of defence should, wherever possible, be the first Line Manager. Sometimes just sharing a problem will relieve it, sometimes some concrete help may be forthcoming. Don't be afraid to take that first step – it could change your life.

A problem shared is a problem halved

Ask yourself

Line Manager

- Do I try too hard to cope on my own?
- Do I encourage my staff to come to me for help?

Trainer

- Do I have the skills to handle one-to-one discussion of stressors?
- Do I make sure group discussion of stress concentrates on the positive as well as the negative aspects?

Welfare Officer

- Do people know about my services?
- What can I do to be more visible?

For all of us

- Have I got the courage to ask for help?

_____

Your notes/personal points

_____

Selected reading

Have a look at the list of organizations at the back of this book.

Getting help for dependency

One of the most noticeable side effects of stress is that we become increasingly dependent on physical 'props'. Such props – alcohol, cigarettes and drugs – increase our level of stress because we know that they aren't doing us any good but we are unable to stop using them because we need them to 'control' our stress. And so we become locked into a vicious circle from which there appears to be no escape.

Why does dependency matter?

Alcohol   Alcohol is a sedative, even though we experience an effect of euphoria and energy when drinking. Light drinking is perfectly okay, providing it is done for enjoyment and not for an artificial lift. (If we need a quick lift then a few moments spent doing a breathing exercise will be far more beneficial.) Heavy drinking is not alcoholism, but it is dangerous because it affects our health and leads to accidents. Alcoholism is an *ILLNESS* and must be treated as such. It is not helpful to castigate alcoholics for their weak will; rather we need to seek medical treatment as we would for any other illness.

Drugs   Drugs are not just the ones which we hear of daily in the press. The most dangerous drugs in this country are the ones we can obtain by prescription, known generically as benzodiazepines. We know them more commonly as Valium, Librium and the like. Such drugs are again okay when used for a short time – perhaps to help us through a bereavement. But their use should be discontinued after two weeks because they are highly addictive. Again, medical treatment will help, and dependents are usually advised to reduce their weekly dosage *slowly* – about half a milligramme each week.

Cigarettes   Cigarettes are strictly speaking a drug because they contain nicotine. Amazing it has been suggested that trying to stop smoking is actually more difficult than coming off heroin! Smoking is particularly associated with work-overload and hence changing the situation may well be an important step for anyone trying to give up cigarettes.

Who can help?

The table that follows gives some ideas that may help, and you will find lists of useful organizations at the back of this booklet. Analysing our environment to find out what is causing us stress (and hence dependency on props) provides a starting point for all of us.

Alcohol and drug dependency can be controlled

Sources of help for alcohol and drug dependency

- Family and friends
- Doctors
- Alcoholics Anonymous
- Stop Smoking Clinics
- Action on Smoking and Health
- Local councils
- Citizens Advice Bureaux
- Acupuncture
- Hypnotherapy
- Health Education Council
- National Council on Alcoholism
- Community Health Councils
- Local hospitals

You can find the addresses of national organizations at the back of this booklet. Your local library will be able to tell you of any local groups and services. Remember, if you need help it *is* available – all you have to do is make the first move.

Ask yourself

For all of us

- Are my drinking/smoking/pill-taking habits still *completely* under my control?

Your notes/personal points

Selected reading

BOOTH, A. L. *Stressmanship.* Chapter 9.

Giving help to others

Together with being willing to ask for help we also need to be prepared to give it, particularly if we have jobs which involve other people. Giving help does not, at least initially, require any special skills or training other than:

- making sure people know we are available
- observing situations and intervening *before* the point of no return
- listening to what people have to say

The art of listening

Listening to what people have to say involves two senses – the eyes and the ears. Very often someone can say one thing but mean another. Unless they are very skilled at keeping their emotions hidden we can usually discern their real meaning by observing their body language as well as hearing the words they are saying. To take an example: someone who is unhappy about a proposed change in their working conditions may not want to tell their manager overtly but will signal their concern by adopting a defensive posture – perhaps keeping their arms tightly folded and not smiling – while still verbally agreeing to the change. So we must involve both our ears and eyes to discern the real messages.

Referral

Whatever the problem it is important that we maintain the confidentiality of the person seeking help. Sometimes the very act of sharing a difficulty may be enough, with others more concrete help will be required. If we can help – perhaps by rearranging work schedules and the like – then we must do so. But we should not fall into the trap of proclaiming an expertise which we do not possess. Sometimes we have to admit that the problem is beyond our scope and refer the person on to an appropriate agency. Referral is not admitting to failure – it is just another way of offering assistance.

Giving help to others is something which we can all do

Ask yourself

Line Manager

- Do I need to develop my own listening skills?
- Do I accept a responsibility to provide help?

Trainer

- What can I do to help course members develop their listening skills?
- Do I know where further help can be obtained?

Welfare Officer

- Do I stress to Line Managers the interface between our roles?

For all of us

- Do I make the time to listen effectively to other people?

Your notes/personal points

Selecting reading

Have a look at the list of useful organizations and individuals who can offer help at the end of this book.

Counselling

Most of us know people to whom others seem to turn in times of crisis. Not because of any special training that they may have had, but simply because they offer a warmth of personality and a listening ear. We can all learn to emulate these people and use them as a model for conducting our relationships. Whether we are Line Managers, Trainers or Welfare Officers, a large part of our work will be concerned with people. Unfortunately we tend to see the Welfare Officer as being the only person involved in counselling; but our staff and trainees should be encouraged to include all three roles in the process of problem-solving.

What can I do?

When people come to us with a problem we have to refrain from getting over-involved. Instead we should be looking for an objective detachment. Over-involvement means that we ourselves may become stressed by the difficulties being expressed, or that we offer our own subjective opinions. Rather, ask open questions to find out more: use 'why', 'what' 'when' and 'how'. Don't be directive, but instead aim for the person to first of all clarify the problem for themselves and then assist them to find their own solutions. Above all, recognize when the problem requires expert assistance and suggest an appropriate next point of call.

Where do I go next?

If the problem is beyond our scope we must be able to direct the person on to someone who can deal with it. Nothing is worse for someone who has finally plucked up the courage to talk about their stress than to find their problem is cursorily dismissed. Normally the Welfare Officer will be able to take up where we have left off. We need to ensure though that the person is aware that our 'listening ear' is still available *and* that we will respect their confidence.

Finally, we don't always have to wait for someone to arrive with problems *before* we tackle them. Taking a proactive role is very important if we want to stop potentially stressful situations from taking hold.

Line Managers, Trainers and Welfare Officers are all involved in the counselling process

Ask yourself

Line Manager

- Do I feel confident in a counselling situation?
- Do my staff feel free to ask me for advice/help?

Trainer

- How can I improve people's problem-solving approaches?
- How do I prevent stressful situations occurring?
- Do I model counselling skills where appropriate in my training events?

Welfare Officer

- Do I encourage people to clarify their own problems?
- Do I always remember to avoid being directive?

For all of us

- Whatever my position, do I need to improve my counselling skills?

Your notes/personal points

Selected reading

OLDFIELD, S. *The counselling relationship: A study of client's experience.* Chapter 7.

Complementary medicine

Complementary medicine – sometimes called alternative medicine – may well have a role to play in the treatment of stress. However, this is not to say that traditional medicine should be ignored. If we are suffering from stress, especially if it has reached the stage where we are affected by physical symptoms such as high blood pressure and ulcers, then it makes sense to use our GP as a starting point. Nowadays many GP's have a much greater awareness of stress, and some are developing a holistic (whole body) approach – which means they are likely to treat not only the physical symptoms but will also explore the reasons behind the symptoms occurring. However, GPs are very busy people and sometimes are unable to devote as much time to patients as they would like, in which case complementary medicine may provide a useful alternative.

Types of complementary medicine

There is a vast range of complementary medicine available. Perhaps the four best-known (and used) are:

Acupuncture which works on the principle that there are a series of energy channels in the body which can become blocked and cause illness. The therapy seeks to open up these channels by stimulation – usually by needles but more recently with electrodes.

Herbalism which uses different parts of plants as a basis for internal and external medicines.

Homeopathy which works on the principle that something which causes symptoms can also cure it.

Chiropractic and osteopathy Both are manipulative therapies which emphasize the treatment of spinal and joint problems.

Do they work?

While there is no scientific evidence that they work there does appear to be a great deal of value if the results of a recent *Which?* survey are anything to go by. Out of a survey of 28,000 people, one in seven had been to a complementary practitioner. A more detailed survey revealed that 74 per cent would go again. The most common problem treated was pain (71 per cent) with 15 per cent being treated for stress-related illness.

Because anyone can set up as a complementary practitioner it makes sense to contact the Institute of Complementary Medicine for assistance in choosing a reputable practitioner. Their address is at the back of this booklet.

Complementary medicines may help if general medicine fails

Improving coping skills

Use the space below to work out an action plan for improving your coping skills.

_____

Being positive – How can I improve?

_____

Relaxing – What relaxation techniques do I want to try?

_____

Fitness and diet – What improvements do I want to make?

_____

Help from outside sources – Where can I go for help/advice?

_____

Selected reading

'Magic or medicine?' in *Which?* October 1986. pp 443–447.

Reducing organizational stress: Job design

In the 1930s the 'scientific management' school propounded the theory that people only worked for money, and that therefore it made sense to break jobs down into a series of exact and timed movements so that people could be rewarded solely on the basis of their productivity. While this approach makes scientific sense, it fails to take into account the multitude of reasons, other than financial reward, why people work.

Repetition and alienation

The legacy of scientific managements is still with us today, although there is much more realization of the complex motivations (self-esteem, responsibility, self-development) which affect performance. An investigation in 1947 discovered that neurotic illness was most pronounced among workers whose job was perceived as boring but required constant attention – such as on an assembly line. Fraser, who headed the inquiry concluded that 'It may be less important to make jobs foolproof than to design them so that they will not be disliked, found boring, or demand long periods of close attention to unvarying detail'.

Work motivation

Subsequent research has tended to confirm Fraser's remarks. * For example, Maslow, Herzberg and MacGregor suggested that job satisfaction depends not only on financial awards and working conditions but also, among other things, on the scope our work provides for variety and involvement. Many of us realize this instinctively. Designing jobs to provide for job satisfaction is one way that we can reduce the likelihood of stress in the workplace.

Designing jobs to provide for job satisfaction is an important way to combat stress

---

*FRASER, R. *The incidence of neurosis amongst factory workers.* Industrial Health Research Board, HMSO. 1947.

Ask yourself

Line Manager

- Do I take all possible steps to make my staff's work interesting and rewarding?
- Am I still clinging to outdated methods or standards?

Trainer

- Do I keep up to date with the changing requirements of people's work?
- Do I cover the full spectrum of motivational factors on management courses?

Welfare Officer

- Are work-related problems increasing in my department?
- What proactive steps should I be taking?

For all of us

- What do I do to improve the way in which my job is carried out?
- Do I accept my own responsibility for forward job planning and work monitoring?

Your notes/personal points

Selected reading

SCOTT, J. and ROCHESTER, A. *Effective management skills: Managing people.* Chapter 5.

Reducing organizational stress: Techniques for better job design

Since most people respond to opportunities for self-enhancement and dislike repetitive and dull tasks, we need to bear two points in mind when designing jobs if we want to get the most from people in terms of performance:

- variety
- involvement

There are two approaches we can take:

- minor modifications to the content of jobs
- major changes to the social and technical environment in which we work

Both are equally valid and one is not exclusive of the other. But, to be really effective, both will have to occur. Some of the approaches are outlined below:

Job rotation Moving employees to different work at the same grade enhances the variety of work while ensuring the work process is undisturbed.

Job enrichment increases the amount of autonomy that we can exercise over the planning and control of our work.

Job involvement asks us to be directly involved in the design of our jobs by such methods as staff appraisal.

Problem solving involves us in finding solutions to workplace difficulties by the use of 'quality circles' and the like.

Some, or all, of these techniques may well prove helpful in alleviating distress. Most require little change in the infra-structure of an organization – or appear to. However, it is likely that we would greet such moves with cynicism and hostility unless they were accompanied by a genuine change in management style. We shall be looking at this in the next pages.

To be effective job design requires variety and involvement

Use the space below to note how you could improve your own job or that of someone who works for you.

Job enrichment

Job involvement

Problem solving

Selected reading

TORRINGTON, D. et al. *Management methods.* pp 91–94.

Management style and communication

As we have seen, people generally require variety and involvement at work to maintain job satisfaction and alleviate distress. Unfortunately, simply redesigning jobs to improve a distressful situation will only work well if the organization encourages an appropriate management style. However, it is sad, but true, that many organizations attempt to tinker around with the mechanism while refusing to attack the central issues of how people are managed.

What is an appropriate management style?

Since the key words are involvement and variety it follows that a traditional, autocratic style is unlikely to produce the right result. It may be possible to increase variety but since this will be *imposed* from the top it will probably do little to improve the situation – indeed it is more likely to encourage resentment and hostility.

If we look at the leadership continuum below, we can see that there is a range of leadership styles available. What is important is selecting an appropriate one, given the circumstances and the human resources. For many people participation leadership reduces stress. However this is only likely to be the case if participation is appropriate given the situation and the preferred styles of both the leader and the lead.

Participation and communication

Increased participation goes hand in hand with effective communication. If people do not know what is happening and why, then the result is further stress. This is particularly ironic if the organization is trying to move from an autocratic to a democratic style – but has not made sure that *everyone* is aware of the shift in emphasis. So, to make the move work we must tell people about it.

We have to encourage an appropriate management style if we are genuinely concerned to alleviate stress

Leadership styles

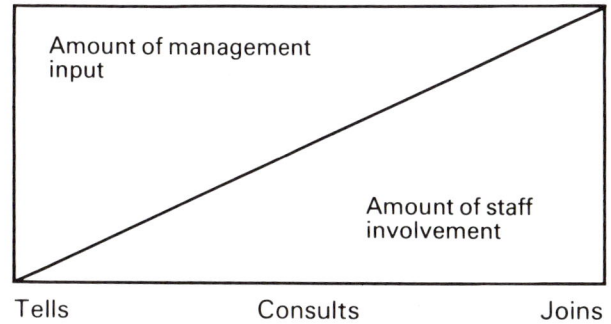

Tells   The manager tells the staff what to do: there is no involvement in decision making.

Consults   The manager consults the staff but still makes the decisions.

Joins   The manager and staff participate to reach a joint decision.

Adapted from TANNENBAUM, R. and SCHMIDT, W. H. 'How to choose a leadership pattern' *Harvard Business Review.* Vol. 36, no. 2, March–April 1985.

Your notes/personal points

Selected reading

SCOTT, J. and ROCHESTER, A. *Effective management skills: Managing people.* pp 122–136.

Tackling change at work

Together with communication, change provides one of the most major work stressors. Most of us fear change; it makes us unsure and uncertain, and until we have actual experience of it we tend not to accept it or welcome it. Introducing workplace change requires sensitivity and involvement at *all* levels if it is to be a success. Imposed change creates unnecessary tension.

A dynamic model of change

However much we might try to avoid it, change is a necessary part of work. Systems, processes and people are not static in an organization, and change occurs daily on at least one of these levels. But, however minor, every change can cause stress unless tackled carefully. It helps to think of change as a dynamic model:

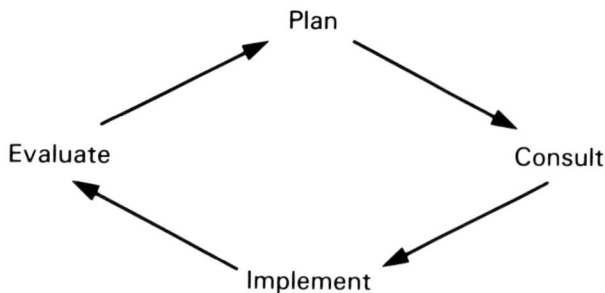

The four stages are self-explanatory, but consultation is the key stage, often left out in our rush to try out a new idea. But consultation is essential to:

- extract underlying fears and hostility
- explain the change fully to allay fears
- modify our plans in the light of increased involvement
- encourage formal and informal debate
- obtain a mandate for change

Only when the issue has been thoroughly explored should we implement the proposed change. Since it is inevitable that the change itself will generate more change we must evaluate it carefully, listening to all contributions, and be prepared to modify our plans yet again – which means returning to the planning stage of our model.

   Of course even using our model will not remove all the suspicions about a proposed change but it will do a great deal to minimize tension for all concerned.

To reduce stress, change should be tackled systematically with the participation of all those involved

Ask yourself

Line Manager

- Am I planning any changes?
- Have I considered how best to involve other people?

Trainer

- How can training minimize the stressful effects of change?
- Do I capitalize on the positive effects of change?

Welfare Officer

- What changes are likely to take place in the near future in the organization or activities of my department?
- How can I help everyone, concerned to prepare for this?

For all of us

- What changes at work are likely to affect me?
- How can I play a full part in effecting the change?

Your notes/personal points

Selected reading

STEWART, V. *Change: Challenge for management.* Chapter 8.

Getting the balance right

As we have continually emphasized, our reactions to stressors are highly individual. No two people will react in precisely the same way to the same event. What we should be aiming for is to avoid moving into the more serious stress responses, but use our initial stress reaction to provide us with the extra energy we need to cope with demands.

Since we all respond differently it follows that we will all find our own ways of coping. It is essential though that we do find those ways – whether it be relaxation, breathing or acupuncture. Improving our general level of health through sensible diet and exercise will increase our chances of stress-proofing. Getting the balance right in all aspects of our lives provides us with the key to using stress positively. We must make stress work *for* us not against us.

Finding out more

During the course of this book we hope to have explored some of the issues about stress and allayed some worries and fears. There is an enormous amount of literature available about the subject, and if you want to find out more the bibliography will direct you. Knowledge itself is a powerful de-stressor. Because the field is constantly changing we would suggest that you use the bibliography as a starting point. Your local library will be able to tell you about new publications which may be of interest.

Section 5.
Further sources of help

Contents

Introduction

This book cannot deal exhaustively with the subject of stress but for your information this section contains details of organizations and individuals who can provide further help and information.

The list is divided by broad subject areas (see below). Each entry gives name, address and, where possible, telephone number and a brief indication of what the organization does.

List of organizations/individuals

Age

Age Concern

Bernard Sunley House
60 Pitcairns Road
Mitcham
Surrey CR4 3LL

081–640 5431

Advice and information for the elderly and those who care for them.

Alcohol

ACCEPT

20 Seagrave Road
London SW6 1RQ

071–381 3155

Counselling, therapy and relaxation training for problem drinkers.

Alcohol Counselling Service

34 Electric Lane
London SW9 8JT

071–737 3579

Provides a direct counselling service.

Alcoholics Anonymous

PO Box 514
11 Redcliffe Gardens
London SW10 9BQ

071–352 9779

2,000 mutual support groups for problem drinkers.

Aquarius

4 St George's Street
Northampton NN1 2TN

0604 32421

Counselling for problem drinkers and their families.

Anorexia

Anorexic Aid

The Priory Centre
11 Priory Road
High Wycombe
Bucks HP13 6SL

0494 21431

A network of self-help groups for anorexics or bulimiacs.

Bereavement

The Compassionate Friends

6 Denmark Street
Bristol BS1 5DQ

0272 292778

Help for bereaved parents.

CRUSE

Cruse House
126 Sheen Road
Richmond
Surrey TW9 1UR

081–940 4818/9047

Organization for widows and their children.

Complementary medicine

British Chiropractic Association

Information Service
5 First Avenue
Chelmsford
Essex CM1 1RX

0245 358487

Provides list of practitioners.

British Homeopathic Association

27A Devonshire Street
London W1N 1RJ

071–935 2163

Provides list of homeopathic practitioners.

British Hypnotherapy Association

67 Upper Berkeley Square
London W1H 7DH

071–723 4443

Provides detailed information, including names of practitioners.

Institute of Complementary Medicine

21 Portland Place
London W1N 3AF

071–636 9543

Information and advice on all aspects of complementary medicine.

Joint Development Resources

24 Cecil Park
Pinner
Middlesex HA5 5HH

081–866 1262

Publications and teaching to control stress, using the Alexander technique.

Osteopaths General Council and Register Ltd

1 Suffolk Street
London SW1Y 4HG

071–839 2060

Provides a list of registered osteopaths (MRO).

Society of Teachers of the Alexander Technique

10 London House
226 Fulham Road
London SW10 9EL

071–351 0828

Provides a list of teachers of the Alexander method (a technique to reduce muscle tension).

Counselling

British Association for Counselling

37A Sheep Street
Rugby
Warwickshire CV21 3BX

0788 78328

Information, advice and publications.

Managers' Counselling Association

Sundridge Park Management College
Plaistow Road
Bromley
Kent BR1 3TP

081–460 8585/8987

Counselling for managers.

Isis Centre

Little Clarendon Street
Oxford OX1 2HS

0865 56648

NHS counselling servce.

Samaritans

See local telephone directory.

Tavistock Clinic

120 Belsize Lane
London NW3 5BA

071–435 7111

Self-referral counselling service for young people aged 16–30. NHS funded.

Depression

Depressives Anonymous

36 Chestnut Avenue
Beverley
North Humberside HU17 9QU

0482 860619

Mutual-help organization, working with medical service.

Depressives Associated

PO Box 5
Castletown
Portland
Dorset DT5 1BQ

Mutual help organization which believes the medical services do not understand depression.

Drugs

ASH

Margaret Pyke House
23–35 Mortimer Street
London W1N 7RJ

071–637 9843

Action on smoking and health.

Families Anonymous

88 Caledonian Road
London N1 9DN

071–227 8805

Self-help for relatives and friends of drug users.

National Tranquiliser Advisory Council (TRANX)

17 Peel Road
Harrow
Middlesex HA3 7QX

081–427 2065

Telephone and personal counselling, and group support.

Health

British Holistic Medical Association

179 Gloucester Place
London NW1 6DX

071–262 5299

Conferences, workshops, lectures and publications.

City Health Care

4–7 Chiswell Street
London EC1Y 4TH

071–638 4988

Established in early 1986, this organization provides a stress management counselling service and guidance on preventative health care. Individual consultation, workshops and seminars are arranged.

College of Health

19 Victoria Park Square
London E2 9PF

081–980 6263

Publishes *Self Health,* a magazine on physical and mental health. Members can ask the college for advice and information.

Devonshire Clinic

21 Devonshire Place
London W1N 1PD

071–935 2565

Integrated health assessments including medical, psychosocial, physiotherapy and occupational assessment to provide a thorough check-up on the health of the whole person. Accepts clients from organizations and individuals.

Institute of Occupational Medicine

8 Roxburgh Place
Edinburgh EH8 9SU

031–667 5131

Multi-disciplinary research into the work environment and health. Contact the librarian for further information.

St Andrew's Hospital

Billing Road
Northampton NN1 5DG

0604 29696

Treatment for stress disorders, including anxiety management, relaxation, social skills training and problem solving.

Women's Health Information Centre

52 Featherstone Street
London EC1Y 8RT

071–251 6580

Information on women's health and self-help groups.

Health and Safety at Work

British Occupational Hygiene Society

1 St Andrew's Place
Regents Park
London NW1 4LB

071–486 4860

Holds conferences and workshops to discuss problems with specific industries and with specific stressors.

Health and Safety Executive

Library and Information Services
Broad Lane
Sheffield S3 7HQ

0742 752539

Information on organizations, regulations etc.

Loneliness

Family Welfare Association

501 Kingsland Road
London E8 4AU

071–254 6251

Support groups in the London area for young mothers and families in distress.

Outsiders Club

PO Box 42B
London W1A 42B

081–741 3332

Social events for those isolated by emotional and physical disability.

Mental health

Good Practices in Mental Health

380–384 Harrow Road
London W9 2HU

071–289 2034

Information on local mental health services.

MIND

22 Harley Street
London W12 2ED

071–637 0741

The National Association for Mental Health. Information and advice.

Phobias

Phobics Society

4 Cheltenham Road
Chorlton-cum-Hardy
Manchester M21 1QN

061–881 1937

Practical help to overcome phobias.

Psychotherapy

Arbours Association

41A Weston Park
London N8 7BU

081–340 7646

Psychotherapy for emotional distress, providing a 'listening ear' telephone service.

Brent Consultation Centre

Johnston House
51 Winchester Avenue
London NW6 7TT

071–328 0918

A free counselling service for young people aged 12–16. Individual psychotherapy for those who live, work or study in Brent.

British Association of Psychotherapy

121 Hendon Lane
London N3 3P3

081–346 1747

Treatment for those having difficult interpersonal relationships.

Institute of Behaviour Therapy

38 Queen Anne Street
London W1M 9LB

081–346 9646

Treats anxiety and depression.

Relaxation

British Wheel of Yoga

Grafton Grange
Grafton
North Yorkshire YO5 9QQ

090 12 3386

Provides list of qualified yoga teachers.

City Relaxation Consultancy

84 Albany Road
Sittingbourne
Kent ME10 1EL

0795 71834

Courses, talks and industrial consultation for stress management and relaxation.

Relaxation for Living

29 Burwood Park Road
Walton-on-Thames
Surrey KT12 5LH

Relaxation classes and correspondence course. Publishes leaflets and tapes. Send large s.a.e. for information.

Yoga for Health Foundation

Ickwell Park
Northill
Nr Biggleswade
Bedfordshire SG18 9EF

Northill (076 727) 271/604/735

Has a residential centre offering stress control, using relaxation techniques.

Self-help

Association of Self-help and Community Groups

7 Chesham Terrace
London W13 9HX

081–579 5589

Runs courses for people who want to set up self-help groups.

Stress

Lifeskills Ltd

3 Brighton Road
London N2 8JU

081–346 9646

Books, tapes and seminars on handling stress.

Organization for Parents Under Stress
29 Newmarket Way
Hornchurch
Essex RM12 6DR

04024 51538

Stress Foundation

Cedar House
Yalding
Kent ME18 6JD

0622 814431

Information, advice and short courses for managers and trainers.

Stress Research and Control Centre

Department of Occupational Psychology
Birkbeck College
University of London
Malet Street
London WC1E 7HX

071–580 6622

071–631 6243

Researches into stress causes and prevention, and provides a service to groups and individuals.

Training

Angela Stern and Associates
(Stress counselling in industry)

11 Palmer Street
London SW1 0AB

071–222 1181

In-house and open courses and seminars.

ASLIB

Information House
26–27 Boswell Street
London WC1N 3JZ

071–430 2671

Occasional stress courses for those in information management.

Don Taylor and Associates Ltd
(Consulting industrial psychologists)

Old Manor House
Venture Road
Chilworth
Southampton SO1 7NP

0703 760639

Seminars and individual counselling on stress management.

Eleanor MacDonald Courses Ltd

4 Mapledale Avenue
Croydon CR0 5TA

081–654 4659

Confidence building and personal effectiveness, with workshop sessions related to stress control.

Greater London Association for Pre-retirement

St Margaret Patten's Church
Eastcheap
London EC3M 1HS

071–623 6630

Professional consultancy for organizers of pre-retirement courses.

Industrial Society

Robert Hyde House
48 Bryanston Square
London W1H 7LN

071–262 2401

Courses and conferences on stress and related subjects.

Industrial Society

Pepperell Unit
Robert Hyde House
48 Bryanston Square
London W1H 7LN

071–262 2401

Courses and workshops on all aspects of stress management.

Jacky Underwood

5 Lower Sheffield
Paul, Penzance
Cornwall TR19 6UH

0736 731126

Short courses and personal consultations for managers under pressure. Training for Trainers.

John Langford Training

30 Tavistock Road
Sheffield S7 1GG

0742 581400

Stress management for organizations and individuals, including stress levels, coping and support structures for change.

Leimon Taylor Consultants

9 Somerset Place
Glasgow G3 7JT

041–333 9576

Courses on stress management in organizations.

Careers and Personal Development Associates Ltd

Career Development Centre
77 Morland Road
Addiscombe
Croydon CR0 6EA

081–654 0808

Provides lists of books, tapes and addresses on managing stress effectively.

Options

19 Belmont Road
Twickenham
Middlesex TW2 5DA

081–755 0133

Personal career development counselling and stress management programme design.

Raphael Centre

Hollander Park
Coldharbour Lane
Hildenborough
Tonbridge
Kent TN11 9LE

0732 833924

Residential centre for individual stress management.

Ron Clements Associates

17 Winchfield Court
Pole Lane
Winchfield
Hants RG27 8BL

025126 4321

Wide interest in stress management and particularly in managers' identifying of stress in their staff.

Skills with People

15 Liberia Road
London N15 1JP

071–359 2370

All aspects of interpersonal skills training, including assertiveness, counselling and stress.

Stress Centres Ltd

101 Harley Street
London W1N 1DF

071–935 1811

Courses related to all aspects of stress.

Women and Training Group

GLOSCAT
Oxstalls House
Gloucester GL2 9HW

0542 426836/7

Workshops and publications related to stress and interpersonal skills.

Section 6.
Bibliography and stress studies

Contents

Introduction

Arrangement

The bibliography is arranged in nine main sections. Sections 1–4 mirror the arrangement of the first four sections in this book, *Understanding Stress – Part One.* They are intended as a useful starting point to sources of further reading for the non-expert. They are not intended to be a comprehensive listing of all the titles available. The entries included have, wherever possible, been chosen for their readability and accessibility by the lay person.

The next three sections are intended to help Line Managers (Section 5), Trainers (Section 6) and Welfare Officers (Section 7).

Section 8 lists a number of stress studies carried out in recent years.

Readers and researchers who wish to find more in-depth material are directed to Section 9, 'Other sources', at the end of this listing.

Entries

Each entry includes:

- author/editor
- title
- publisher
- date of publication
- ISBN where allocated

Many entries also include a brief summary to help you decide if the title is useful for your needs.

Main sections

1. What is stress?   **NB** Since readers will find both the definition of stress and its symptoms included as part of virtually all works dealing with stress these sections are necessarily brief.
2. Symptoms of stress

3. Causes of stress   Organizational stressors
   Personal stressors
   Social stressors

4. Managing stress   Assertiveness
   and coping   Attitudes/beliefs
                       Avoidance techniques
                       Complementary
                         medicine
                       General
                       Organizational approach
                       Relaxation
                       Time management

5. Role of the Line   Identification
   Manager   Causes
                      Managing
                      Consequences

6. Role of the Trainer   Interpersonal skills
                         Strategies

7. Role of the Welfare   Counselling
   Officer   Strategies

8. Stress studies   General
                    Industry
                    Service organizations
                      (including the Civil
                      Service)
                    Women

9. Other sources

Bibliography

1. What is stress?

BOOTH, A. L.
Stressmanship
Severn House
1985
0727820540

Explains what stress is and how to manage it to good, rather than harmful, effect.

CONSUMERS ASSOCIATION
'Feeling stressed?'
Which?
September 1986
pp 419–422

Examines stress as part of normal life and how too much stress can affect health and coping ability. Provides a stress analysis questionnaire and tips on how to deal with excessive stress.

COOPER, C.
'What's new in stress?'
Personnel Management
June 1984
pp 40–43

FRIEDMAN, M. D. and ROSENMAN, R. H.
Type 'A' behaviour and your heart
Wildwood House
1975
0704501589

Suggests that behaviour is the single most important factor in causing heart disease.

HARRIS, A. B.
Breakpoint: Stress and the crisis of modern living
Turnstone Books
1979
0855000937

Produces a general theory of evolutionary crisis and suggests we have to recreate our environment so that it is compatible with our genetic nature.

NOTTIDGE, P. and LAMPLUGH, D.
Stress and overstress
Angus and Robertson
1974
020795528X

2. Symptoms of stress

EDMUNDS, L.
'How to look for the tell-tale signs of stress'
Daily Telegraph
3 February 1984
p17

HOLMES, T. H. and RAHE, R. H.
'The social readjustment rating scale'
Journal of Psychosomatic Research
1967
pp 213–218

Describes life events, their stress related effect and build-up in the individual.

NELSON, D. L. and QUICK, J. C.
'Professional women: Are distress and disease inevitable?'
Academy of Management Review
Vol. 10, no. 2, April 1985
pp 206–218

TRICK, Dr K. L. K.
'The tell-tale signs of executive stress'
The Director
July 1984
p 76

Describes physical and behavioural symptoms.

3. Causes of stress

Organizational stressors

BEEHR, T. A. and BHAGAT, R. S. ed.
Human stress and cognition in organizations: an integrated perspective
Wiley
1985
0471869546

BROCK, P.
'Stress at work has now reached epidemic proportions'
The Guardian
13 November 1985
p 13

COOPER, C. L. and MARSHALL, J.
Understanding executive stress
Macmillan Press
1978
0333197917

Based on research, this book examines the fit between the manager, the organization and the wider environment.

COOPER, C. L. and PAYNE, R. ed.
Stress at work
John Wiley
1978
0471995479

Outlines the main areas of research, prevention and treatment of stress at work.

CURSON, C. ed.
Flexible patterns of work
Institute of Personnel Management
1986
0852923767

Includes a discussion on flexible working hours.

EVERLY, G. S.
The stress mess solution
Prentice Hall
1980
087619434X

Causes and solutions of workplace stress.

KEARNS, J. L.
Stress in industry
Priory Press
1973
0850780543

Analyses aspects of work stress and suggests how it can be tackled.

KOWALSKI, A.
'Stress in the workplace can cost you big money'
Canadian industrial relations and personnel developments
Vol. 26, no. 2, March 1979
pp 18–22

Makes a case for implementing organizational stress reduction programmes.

LEVI, L.
Stress in industry: Causes, effects and prevention
International Labour Organisation
1984
9221035395

A brief introduction, from an international perspective, to workplace stress.

MCDONALD, N. and DOYLE, M.
The stresses of work
Van Nostrand Reinhold
1982
0442307381

Examines work stressors, including low pay, shift work, job design and work organisation.

MURRELL, H.
Work stress and mental strain
Department of Employment. WRU Occasional Paper 67.
1978

A survey reviewing the literature on work stress and mental strain. Includes an extensive bibliography.

NEWTON, T. J. and KEENAN, A.
'Coping with work-related stress'
Human relations
Vol. 38, no. 2, February 1985
pp 107–126

Working women
TUC
1983
0900878924

Looks at the lives of working women. Designed to provide discussion briefs for Trainers, shop-stewards and women's groups.

Personal stressors

DAVIDSON, M. and COOPER, C. L.
'The extra pressures on women executives'
Personnel Management
June 1980
pp 48–51

LAKE, T.
Living with grief
Sheldon Press
1984
0859694267

Describes the different aspects of grief and suggests ways of working it through so that the result is a deeper awareness of the values of life.

LAKE, T.
Loneliness: Why it happens and how to overcome it
Sheldon Press
1980
085969285X

NIXON, P. G. F.
'Stress, lifestyle and cardiovascular disease: a cardiological odyssey'
British Journal of Holistic Medicine
Vo. 1, 1984
pp 20–29

PARKES, C. M.
Bereavement: Studies of grief in adult life
2nd edition
Penguin
1986
0140226451

The standard British work on bereavement, describes the response to bereavement and methods of coping.

PIKE, M.
Long life: Expectations of old age
J M Dent
1980
0460022113

Focuses on the everyday life of the elderly, on practical problems and how they can be overcome to live life to the full.

Social stressors

BARON, R. A.
The tyranny of noise
Harper and Row
1971

Summary of the stressor effects of different types of noise in modern society. Includes statistics of effects on health and means of minimising noise.

BOOTH, A. L. ed.
Stress
Stress Syndrome Foundation
1982
0946029008

Conference proceedings providing an introduction to stress in industry and modern society.

COCHRANE, R. and ROBERTSON, A.
'The life events inventory: a measure of the relative severity of psycho-social stressors'
Journal of Psychosomatic Research
1973
pp 135–139

Follows on from the work of Holmes and Rahe and provides a list of change events together with their stress rating.

CONSUMER'S ASSOCIATION
Living with stress
Hodder
1982
0340274867

HALSEY, A. H.
Change in British society
3rd edition
OUP
1986
0192892002

Overview of technological and social change.

KING, J. and STOTT, M. ed.
Is this your life
Virago
1977
0704338041

Investigates the attitudes and images about women presented to us by the media.

TOFFLER, A.
Future shock
Bodley Head
1970
0370013018

Examines the pace of change in society and suggests we need to be better prepared to cope.

WRIGHT, H. B.
Ease and dis-ease: How to achieve permanent good health
Longman Professional
1986
0851212301

Advice on achieving life-long health by altering one's lifestyle to reduce stress.

4. Managing stress

Assertiveness

BACK, K. and BACK, K.
Assertiveness at work: A practical guide to handling awkward situations
McGraw-Hill
1982
007084576X

Puts forward techniques for dealing successfully with awkward people and situations at work.

LINEHAM, M. and EGAN, K.
Asserting yourself
Century
1983
0712600841

A practical guide to assertion.

Attitudes/beliefs

COLEMAN, V.
Mindpower
Century
1986
0712612009

How to use your mind to heal the body.

HOWARD, R. W.
Coping and adapting: How you can learn to cope with stress
Angus and Robertson
1985
0207149461

Shows that coping skills can be developed as other learned skills and stressors handled in a positive way.

SHARPE, R. and LEWIS, D.
Thrive on stress: How to make it work to your advantage
Souvenir Press
1977
0285622528

Avoidance techniques

CHAITOW, L.
Your complete stress-proofing programme
Thorsons
1984
0722509839

How to protect yourself against the ill-effects of stress, including relaxation and meditation.

FRIEDMAN, M. and ULMER, D.
Treating Type 'A' behaviour: You and your heart
Michael Joseph
1985
0718125665

Examines the origins and diagnosis of Type 'A' behaviour and includes a practical treatment programme to alter behaviour.

GOODIN, M.
'Is smoking killing your staff?'
Personnel Resource Management [now *Leadership*]
Vol. 2, no. 4, September 1986, Ardent Publications
pp 15–17

Examines smoking as a workplace hazard and the benefits, including cost benefit of a smoke-free working environment.

Why Harry?
Medical Advisory Service of the Northern Ireland Civil Service

A pamphlet emphasising the value of exercise in preventing coronary heart disease.

Complementary medicine

INGLIS, B.
The Book of the Back
Ebury Press
1978
0852231334

Examines the options and risks of orthodox and non-orthodox treatment.

INGLIS, B. and WEST, R.
The alternative health guide
Michael Joseph
1983
0718121856

A comprehensive guide to alternative therapies.

'Magic or medicine?'
Which?
October 1986
pp 443–447

Examines complementary medicine, including acupuncture, homeopthy and osteopathy.

SLEET, R.
Hypnotherapy: A patient's guide
Element
1983
0906540402

Explains the practice of hypnotherapy and advises on choosing a hypnotherapist. Includes a chapter on anxiety and tension.

General

BEECH, H. R.
A behavioural approach to the management of stress: A practical guide to techniques
Wiley
1982
0471100544

BRETON, S.
Don't panic: A guide to overcoming panic attacks
Macdonald Optima
1986
0356144518

A self-help guide including tables, diagrams and questionnaires.

COLEMAN, V.
Stress and your stomach
Sheldon Press
1983
0859693759

A self-help guide.

COOPER, C. L.
Stress check
Prentice-Hall
1981
013852632X

Coping with the stressors of life and work.

KARLINS, M. and ANDREWS, L. M.
Biofeedback
Lippinscott
1982

An introduction to monitoring stress through the use of biofeedback.

LANOIL, G. WITKIN
Coping with stress: A practical self help guide for women
Revised edition
Sheldon
1985
0859694380

A practical self-help guide for women.

LEECH, K.
What everyone should know about drugs
Sheldon Press
1983
0859693740

Sets out causes and symptoms associated with drugs and advice on prevention and cure.

McCLEAN, A. A.
High tech survival kit: managing your stress
Wiley
1986
0471840033

McCLEAN, A. A.
Work stress
Addison Wesley
1979
0201045923

MORSE, D. R. and FURST, L.
Stress for success
Van Nostrand Reinhold
1982
0442262280

A holistic approach to stress management.

RUSH, J.
Beating depression
Century
1983
0712600825

A summary of the history, symptoms, causes and treatment with advice about seeking help.

SELYE, H.
Stress without distress
Corgi
1987
0552130028

Suggests 'altruistic egoism' cushions the harmful effects of stress.

'Stress special'
Good Housekeeping
November 1986
pp 113–138

Describes stress and stress-alleviating therapies.

THOMPSON, K. and TUNSTALL, J. ed.
Sociological perspectives: Selected readings
Penguin for Open University Press
pp 220–233
1971
0140806083

Organizational approach

BENNER, P. E.
Stress and satisfaction on the job
Praeger
1984
0030638399

Coping with work stress during mid-career.

CAMERON, C. and ELUSORR, S.
Thank God it's Monday: Strategies for increasing job satisfaction
Ebury Press
1986
0852235798

Offers practical strategies to help anyone get the 'perfect' job or get more satisfaction from their present one.

FRANCIS, D.
Managing your own career
Fontana
1985
0006368727

A self-help pack for those seeking to improve the quality of their working lives. Includes questionnaires and case-studies.

LUCAS, M.
How to survive the 9 to 5
Thames Methuen
1986
0423019309

An overview of stress at work, including definition and diagnosis, with the emphasis on coping.

'Planning for retirement'
Management Today
November 1986
pp 125–126

Report of a seminar on retirement planning for senior executives.

'Stress'
Prison Service News
February 1987
pp 4–5

A two-page guide to stress and coping.

WHITE, G.
Managing stress in organisational change
ACAS/Work Research Unit
1984
Occasional Paper 31

Describes strategies for reducing pressures during the process of organisational change.

Relaxation

BIBBY, C.
'Relax! for your heart's sake'
Training Officer
January 1986
pp 17–19

Describes relaxation sessions using biofeedback.

HORN, S.
Relaxation: A self-help guide to the prevention and control of stress-related illness
Thorsons
1986
0722511876

A self-help guide to the prevention and control of stress-related disease.

KIRSTA, A.
The book of stress survival: How to relax and de-stress your life
Allen and Unwin
1986
0041320220

MADDERS, J.
Stress and relaxation: How to cope with stress and nervous tension, insomnia, migraine and high blood pressure
Martin Dunitz: Macdonald Orbis
1979
0906348005

SELIGER, SUSAN
Stop killing yourself
Exley
1986
1850150605

STEPHEN, J.
'Relaxing practices'
New Society
2 May 1986. Vol. 76
p 22

Describes a scheme to help with tensions and stress at work.

Time management

LANE, C.
'How to get time on your side'
Industrial and Commercial Training
Vol. 17, no. 6, 1985
pp 10–11

Describes a technique to help managers control stress by managing their time more effectively.

LANE, C.
'How to manage stress'
Management today
September 1985
pp 74–76

Describes various time-management techniques to minimise managerial stress.

NOON, J.
'A' time: The busy manager's action plan for effective self-management
Van Nostrand Reinhold
1985
0442306423

Describes techniques for saving up to 20 per cent of work time and converting it to more profitable and effective performance.

5. Role of the Line Manager

Identification

GOODWIN, R.
Stress at work
Chester House Publications
1976
0715000632

Introductions to organizational stressors, drawing upon studies on groups of supervisors in two companies.

GOWLER, D. and LEGGE, K. (ed.)
Managerial stress
Gower
1975
0716102773

IVANCEVICH, J. M. and MATTESON, M. T.
Stress and work: a managerial perspective
Scott, Foresman
1980
0673153819

Integrates stress theory, research and application from different disciplines to provide managers with a framework for examining work stress.

NORFOLK, D.
Executive stress
Revised edition of *Stress factor*
Arrow Books
1986
0099457806

How to recognize the danger signals of over-stress and how to harness stress for positive benefit.

Causes

BLOTNICK, S.
Otherwise engaged
Facts on file, U. S.
1986
0816010935

The results of a 25-year survey on 3,000 career women, exploring the underlying pressures which have caused them to sabotage their own efforts to achieve.

COOPER, C. L. and MARSHALL, J.
Understanding executive stress
Macmillan Press
1978
0333197917

Analyses the fit between the person and the work environment and external sources of stress arriving from social and family life.

DAVIDSON, M. J.
'The problems faced by female supervisors'
Supervisory Management
Vol. 37, no. 1, 1986
pp 5–10

Describes the factors in the supervisor's role which women supervisors find the most stressful.

McDONALD, N. and DOYLE, M.
The stresses of work
Van Nostrand Reinhold
1982
0442307381

Focuses on social and psychological factors at work which cause stress and seeks to place the issue on the trade union negotiating table.

McGREGOR, D.
The human side of enterprise
McGraw-Hill
1985
0070450986

Examines the effect of managerial style on performance and motivation.

STEWART, V.
Change: challenge for management
McGraw-Hill
1983
0070845999

Examines the forces for coping with and accepting change.

Managing stress

ADAIR, J.
Effective team building
Gower
1986
0566026058

Includes examples, exercises, case studies and checklists.

BLANCHARD, M. and TAGER, M.J.
Working well: managing for health and high performance
Gower (hardback)
1986
0566826813

Wildwood House (paperback)
1986
0704505428

Introduces the PERKS system–*Participation, Environment, Recognition, Knowledge* and *Style.*

BOARD, R. DE.
Counselling people at work: an introduction for managers
Gower
1983
0566023768

Examines problems encountered by people at work and the effectiveness of a non-directive approach in tackling problems.

The effective manager: a resource handbook
Local Government Training Board
1986
0903994135

Provides managers with modular material to facilitate training, including *Stress and the manager.*

MUIR, J.
'Managing change'
British Journal of Administrative Management
Vol. 1, November 1986
pp 8–10

Looks at strategies for change, particularly in relation to redundancy. Argues consultation is the key.

PARSON, M.
An executive's coaching handbook
Facts on File, US
1986
0816011648

Techniques for everyday personnel management, includes sections on delegation, alcoholism and drug abuse.

RICKARDS, T.
Problem solving through creative analysis
Gower
1974
0716102145

A detailed, practical introduction to problem solving methods supported by illustrative case studies.

SCOTT, J. and ROCHESTER, A.
Effective management skills: managing people
Sphere/British Institute of Management
1984
0722176317

STUBBS, D.
Assertiveness at work
Pan
1986
0330292315

Aimed at managers, this book examines the skills involved in good relationships and effective managerial communication.

TANNENBAUM, R. and SCHMIDT, W. H.
'How to choose a leadership pattern'
Harvard Business Review
Vol. 36, no. 2, March–April 1958

TORRINGTON, D. et. al.
Management methods
Gower (hardback)
1985
05660266406

IPM (paperback)
1985
0852923554

A manual for managers containing 50 action plans for managing different situations.

TRUESDALE, V.
'Your stress levels and the management of work'
Taxes
February 1986
pp 6–8

Examines how we react to stress and offers ideas on managing workloads, assuming an overload.

Consequences

ALBRECHT, K.
Stress and the manager: how to make it work for you
Prentice-Hall
1979
0138526818

Self-help guide to using stress positively.

IVANCEVICH, J. M. et al.
'Who's liable for stress on the job'
Harvard Business Review
March–April 1985
Vol. 63, no. 2,
pp 60–72

Examines stress related law suits in the United States and suggests managers should be able to identify and remove potential stressors to avoid litigation.

MELHUISH, A.
'Are you working too hard to be efficient?'
Director
Vol. 40, no. 5,
December 1986
p 85

Argues that long working hours may decrease rather than increase efficiency.

6. Role of the Trainer

Interpersonal Skills

ACKROYD, A. (ed.)
Training counselling
British Association for Counselling
1984
0946181136

Lists counselling training courses available in the UK

COOPER, C. L. (ed.)
Improving interpersonal relations: some approaches to social skills training
Gower
1981
056602277X

COOPER, G., CRAWFORD, C. et al.
Trainers in counselling
British Association for Counselling
1984
094618111X

Lists Trainers specialising in counselling. Loose leaf format with an amendment service.

HONEY, P.
Face-to-face: a practical guide to interactive skills
Institute of Personnel Management
1976
085292142X

INSKIPP, F.
A manual for Trainers: resource book for setting up and running counselling courses
Alexia Publications
1985
0951095005

PAUL, N.
'Assertiveness without tears: a training programme for executive equality'
Personnel Management
Vol. 11, no. 41
April 1979
pp 37–40

Strategies

BOND, M. and KILTY, J.
Practical methods of dealing with stress
Human Potential Research Project, Department of Educational Studies, University of Surrey
1982
1852370114

Resource material and workshop outlines.

BOOT, N. BUCLE, A. and PERKINS, E.
The stress pack
Nottingham and Bassetlaw Health Education Unit
1986

A pack for Trainers to use with individuals and groups. Includes OHP slides and handouts.

The cost of stress: summary of a one-day workshop
Women in Training, c/o Department of Management Studies,
Gloucestershire College of Arts and Technology, Oxstalls Lane, Gloucester
GL2 9HW
1984

Includes papers on the cost of stress, causes, managerial stress and coping.

COX, S.
Change and stress in the modern office
Further Education Unit/Pickup, Department of Education and Science
1986
0948621427

Analyses the changing office environment and identifies training needs and solutions.

Counselling for resettlement: dealing with stress
Training Section, Agricultural and Food Research Council
September 1986

Defines stress and suggests coping skills.

McCLEAN, A. A.
Work stress
Addison Wesley
1979
0201045923

ORLANS, V.
'The Trainer's role in stress management and prevention'
Journal of European and Industrial Training
Vol. 10, no. 5, 1986
pp 3–5

Examines effects of workplace stress and absenteeism. Suggests training programmes should analyse individual/occupational/organizational stressors and play a proactive role in managing stress.

7. Role of the Welfare Officer

Counselling

BREESE, J. (ed.)
Counselling resources directory
British Association for Counselling
1986/7
0946181179

Loose-leaf format bringing together information about counselling organizations and individuals by geographical area.

GELLERMAN, S. W.
'A way to save an executive: on-site counselling'
Personnel
Vol. 62, no. 6, June 1985
pp 55–60

An approach to assist executives who cannot work well with other people.

MEGRANAHAN, M.
'Counselling at work'
Journal of General Management
Vol. 11, no. 1, Autumn 1985
pp 61–67

Argues that counsellors are agents for change

OLDFIELD, S.
The counselling relationship: a study of client's experience
Routledge and Kegan Paul
1983
0710094221

Concerned with both the theory and practice of counselling.

WATTS, A. G., (ed.)
Counselling at work: papers presented by a working party of the Standing Conference for the Advancement of Counselling
Bedford Square Press
1977
0719909252

Strategies

ALLAN, G. A.
A sociology of friendship and kinship
Allen and Unwin
1979
0043011055

ARGYLE, M. (ed.)
Social skills and work
Methuen
1981
0416730000

CONSUMERS ASSOCIATION
Understanding mental health
Hodder
1986
0340381612

Includes chapters on recognising and coping with stress and describes the roles of professional carers and support organizations.

DIXON, A.
Dealing with drugs
BBC
1987
0563211350

Aimed at social workers and others in the caring profession this provides background information on drugs, their effects and ways of dealing with addiction.

DOYLE, C.
'Stamping out second-hand cigarettes'
Daily Telegraph
2 February 1987
p 16

Describes workplace smoking policies and the hazards that face the passive smoker.

INSTITUTE OF COMPLEMENTARY MEDICINE (ICM)
The ICM complementary medicine yearbook
Foulsham
1987
0572014090

A directory of UK practices, therapies and information. Includes addresses.

LACEY, R. and WOODWARD, S.
'That's life!' survey and tranquillisers
BBC
1985
0563202947

Describes the longest UK survey undertaken on tranquillisers and includes advice on giving up and finding help.

OSTELL, A.
'Where stress screening falls short'
Personnel Management
September 1986
pp 34–37

Discusses practical steps to establish a screening and treatment service for stressed employees.

RADFORD, T.
'Relaxation: a fresh approach to efficiency?'
Welfare news
Cabinet Office (MPO)
August 1986
pp 8–10

Describes a series of relaxation classes held for staff in the Forestry Commission.

SMITH, P. B.
Group processes and personal change
Harper and Row
1980
0063181517

8. Stress studies

Stress research in the Civil Service

The Civil Service Occupational Health Service (CSOHS) has been interested in stress in the Civil Service for some years and has helped conduct, or been associated with, a number of research projects. A good deal of the data which is so often quoted, in this context was derived from the so-called 'Whitehall Study' set up in 1968 to look into factors which prevent cardio-respiratory disease in male civil servants. This involved some 18,000 men aged 40 to 64. It was followed up in 1978 by a study involving 1,200 male and female employees in the Department of the Environment.

The most interesting finding was that those at greater risk from illnesses which are thought to be stress-related – primarily coronary heart disease and raised blood pressure – were the lower level civil servants at messengerial and clerical level. Messengers had a coronary heart disease rate 3.6 times that of those in the higher Civil Service, and this was not adequately explained by other factors like differences in smoking habits.

Other recent research has been carried out by Professor Cary Cooper of University of Manchester Institute of Science and Technology into stress among Tax Officers (Higher Grade) in the Inland Revenue. This research was primarily conducted for the Inland Revenue Staff Federation. It suggested that Tax Officers are more prone to anxiety and depression, than those at comparable levels in other professions.

The CSOHS is currently helping Professor Michael Marmot of the Department of Community Medicine in the University College Hospital Medical School conduct an extended study in six departments of stress-related problems and different approaches to dealing with them.

General

CHERRY, N.
'Nervous strain, anxiety and symptoms amongst 32-year-old men at work in Britain'
Journal of Occupational Psychology
Vol. 57, no. 2, 1984
pp 95–105.

GILES, E.
Stress and the personal director: a preliminary investigation
1985

A research project which includes questionnaires and a bibliography.

Apply Murray Giles Associates, 1 Rectory Place, Hawkswood Lane, Chislehurst, Kent BR7 5PN.

MCDERMOTT, D.
'Professional burnout and its relation to job characteristics, satisfactions and control'
Journal of Human Stress
Vol. 10, no. 2, Summer 1984
pp 79–85

A study which examines work burnout among 104 professionals. Concludes that there is significant correlation between the amount of work control by the individual and burnout.

ORLANS, V. and SHIPLEY, P.
A survey of stress management and prevention facilities in a sample of UK organizations
Department of Occupational Psychology, Birkbeck College, University of London
1983

Examines stress control in 35 organizations with particular focus on training and welfare. Concludes that only a few tackle stress directly with the emphasis on management rather than prevention.

Industry

BURKE, R. J.
'Are you fed up with work?'
Personnel Administration
Vol. 34, no. 1, January/February 1971
pp 27–31

Identifies methods of managing job tensions among supervisors of engineering personnel.

FRASER, R.
The incidence of neurosis among factory workers
HMSO
Report no. 90, Industrial Health Research Board, Medical Research Council
1947

Examines the incidence of neurosis among 3,000 employees in light and medium engineering factories, over a six-month period. Work factors emerge as being an important cause of neurotic illness.

MARSHALL, J. and COOPER, C. L. (ed.)
Coping with stress at work: case studies from industry
Gower
1981
0566023385

An account of how different organizations are responding to the effects of stress, including training, relaxation, organizational structure etc.

Service organizations (including the Civil Service)

COOPER, C. L.
'Stress in the Police Service'
Journal of Occupational Medicine
Vol. 24, no. 9, 1982
pp 653–655

COOPER, C. L.
Mental health and satisfaction among Tax Officers
Department of Management Sciences. UMIST
1984/5

Assessed the mental well-being of 318 tax officers. Found that an autocratic management style predicted job dissatisfaction.

CRUMP, J., COOPER, C. L. and MAXWELL, V. B.
'Stress among Air Traffic Controllers: Occupational sources of coronary heart disease risk'
Journal of Occupational Behaviour
Vol. 2, no. 4, 1981
pp 293–303

FARBER, B. A.
Stress and burnout in the human service professions
Pergamon Press
1983
0080288014

A preliminary study of stress in the Police Service: Conclusions and recommendations as submitted to the Association of Chief Police Officers working party on police stress
SRDB Human Factors Group, Home Office.
1983.
Final report of a workshop series which includes management systems, styles and support.

'Stress in the medical laboratory'
Medical Laboratory Sciences
Vol. 43, Supplement 1, October 1986
pp 583–84
Biochemistry Department
St. Vincents Hospital, Elm Park, Dublin 4

Measures occupational stress of hospital personnel. Finds that very small and very large laboratories are equally stressful.

ZALEZNIK, A. et al.
'Stress reactions in organisations: Syndrome, causes and consequences'
Behavioural Science
Vol. 22, no. 3, May 1977
pp 151–162

A study of stress among 2,000 individuals in a large organization in Canada.

Printed in the United Kingdom for HMSO.
Dd.295079, C10, 9/92, 3397/5, 5673, 210366.

Women

COOPER, C. L. and DAVIDSON, M. J.
High pressure: working lives of women managers
Fontana
1982
0006362362

Suggests that women managers have major additional stressors to cope with at work and at home.

COOPER, C. L. and DAVIDSON, M. J.
Stress and the woman manager
Robertson
1983
0855206233

Compares managerial men and women and concludes that, while women can help themselves, direct action is required in organizations on recruitment, training and career counselling.

HAYNES, S. G. and FEINLEIB, M.
'Women, work and coronary heart disease'
American Journal of Public Health
Vol. 70, no. 2, 1980
pp 133–141

TUNG, R. L.
'Comparative analysis of the occupational stress profiles of male versus female administrators'
Journal of Vocational Behaviour
Vol. 17, 1980
pp 344–355

A study which suggests that female administrators experience substantially lower levels of self-perceived work stress than their male counterparts.

9. Other sources

There are a number of organizations offering bibliographic information. Two we have found particularly useful are:

1. ACAS
   Work Research Unit
   St Vincent House
   30 Orange Street
   London WC2H 7HH
   071–839 9281

Publishes a bibliography entitled *Workplace stress* with regular updates. Non-annotated.

2. John Chittock
   37 Gower Street
   London WC1E 6HH
   071–580 2842

Publishes *Stress: a resources file,* which includes courses, publications and research.